A Little Out of The Ordinary

Daily Reflections for Ordinary Time

John J. McIlhon

A Liturgical Press Book

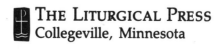

THE LITURGICAL PRESS
Collegeville, Minnesota

Cover design by Ann Blattner.

1   2   3   4   5   6   7   8

Library of Congress Cataloging-in-Publication Data

McIlhon, John.
    A little out of the ordinary : daily reflections for ordinary time
    / John J. McIlhon.
        p.   cm.
    ISBN 0-8146-2274-7
    1. Church year meditations.   2. Christian life—Catholic authors.
    I. Title.
    BX2170.C55M4   1994
    242'.2—dc20   93-40564
                                                                   CIP

Contents

Preface

As Jesus approaches Jerusalem, he weeps, "You failed to recognize the time of your visitation" (Luke 19:44). He weeps because *he* is their "visitation" in the ordinary events of daily life. He visits them in the same way that caused his own mother to say, "My being proclaims the greatness of the Lord, . . . for he has looked upon his servant in her lowliness" (Luke 1:46, 48).

Mary's proclamation of the Lord's "greatness" in her "lowliness" is the humility that acknowledges that we are all "a little out of the ordinary," which the Lord chooses to visit and there to find a home with us. We see his daily visitations with the eyes of faith, which acknowledges that ordinary lives can become miracles of joy.

This book, *A Little out of the Ordinary,* follows four books of reflections—on the mysteries of Advent, Christmas, Lent, and Easter. It proposes that these mysteries, hidden in the ordinary time of our lives, seek to visit us and cause us to reflect with Mary, "God who is mighty has done great things for me" (Luke 1:49). These mysteries ask to be invested in our humanity in exchange for our investiture in God's divinity, an exchange that happens, little by little, in ordinary time.

To incorporate thirty-four weeks of daily reflections, it has been my task to make each reflection "a little out of the ordinary." I have followed the pattern of Word, Reflection, and Question for Your Reflection that I used in the four previous books: Advent's *God is with Us,* Christmas's *O Marvelous Exchange,* Lent's *Forty Days Plus Three,* and Easter's *Fifty Days Plus Forever.*

This book of reflections suggests that God's mysteries are not at home with the mystique of God "out there." From their hiddenness they seek our identity for Christ's ongoing incarnation. God's mysteries are not conversation pieces; rather, they are the promise of substance for

5

ordinary lives created in the likeness of God's image. Like us in all things except sin, Jesus chooses to be at home in the littleness of ordinary lives, enabling all men and women to sing with Mary, "My being proclaims the greatness of the Lord" (Luke 1:46).

John J. McIlhon

First Week in Ordinary Time

WORD

"All wisdom comes from the LORD
and with him it remains forever" (Sir 1:1).

REFLECTION

As a small child I prayed dally for an apparition. Instead God granted me the wisdom to see his presence in all of creation.

In a beautiful prayer, St. Clement sees Jesus as God's Wisdom. He writes: "You formed your creation with wisdom, established it with prudence. Everything we see proclaims your goodness" (St. Clement I, pope).[1]

Wisdom is the vision that sees creation's goodness reflecting God's presence. It sees with "the eyes of [our] heart"[2] the grandeur of God everywhere. Wisdom is God's gift of looking into the depths of creation with the *expectation* of experiencing its power to proclaim God's goodness.

Those who see beyond what eyes perceive give evidence that Christ, the Wisdom of God, is fully active within them.

QUESTION FOR YOUR REFLECTION

What is greater, knowledge or wisdom? Why?

WORD

"What, I ask, is more pleasing than the beauty of God?"
(St. Basil the Great, bishop).[3]

REFLECTION

St. Basil the Great defines sin as "the misuse of powers given us by God for doing good, a use contrary to God's commandments."[4] This "misuse" is often twisted to justify human existence. It justifies the accumulation of this earth's goods as the reason why we exist.

Such justification lacks wisdom! If wisdom permits us to see *how* and *what* God sees, then another criterion appears for determining the worth of human life. Wisdom allows us to see this earth's goods not as lesser gods of self-indulgence but as sacraments of God's presence.

Wisdom asks that reason be the companion of faith. In this marriage of heaven and earth, we become the home for God's incomprehensibility. Wisdom with faith graces reason to see the beauty of God in all things and persuades us to act accordingly. We see the reason for sinlessness!

QUESTION FOR YOUR REFLECTION

What is contemplation?

WEDNESDAY

WORD

"Through creation itself the Word reveals God the Creator" (St. Irenaeus, bishop).[5]

REFLECTION

Wisdom is not the accumulation of knowledge. It is the graced capacity of peering through faith's door to touch God's identity.

Wisdom is both uncreated and created. It is the uncreated presence of God's Word indelibly marked on our humanity. "The Father," writes St. Iranaeus, "is beyond our sight and comprehension; but he is known by his Word, who tells us of him who is beyond all telling."[6]

Wisdom is also created, because through us, with us, and in us "the Word reveals God the Creator." Jesus is clothed with humanity so that uncreated Wisdom might declare the wonders of God "to the ends of the world" (Ps 19:5).

All who humbly accept God's Word about the dignity of creation are graced to gaze beyond creation's limitations. With Wisdom's eye they see that "through creation itself the Word reveals God the Creator."

QUESTION FOR YOUR REFLECTION

How is concern for a nation's environment a sign of wisdom?

THURSDAY

WORD

"As the rising sun is clear to all, so the glory of the LORD fills all his works" (Sir 42:16).

REFLECTION

God's Wisdom is more than the light of a trillion suns. Christ comes as the presence of Wisdom's light. Like the sun that reveals earth's beauty, the Son of God reveals the beauty of human dignity once hidden in the darkness of Adam's decision to choose delusion over light.

The brilliance of the sun is darkness compared to the light of God's Wisdom. This Wisdom is the Word of God ever proclaiming, "I am the light of the world" (John 8:12). "This is the Word that created this whole world and enlightens it by his loving wisdom" (St. Athanasius, bishop).[7]

How comic to measure the light of the sun by the flame of a candle. How tragic to measure God's Wisdom by the light of a technology asserted to be reason's ultimate glory. The light of God's Wisdom enables us to see the meaning of human existence in the light of humanity's *being* in the likeness to God.

QUESTION FOR YOUR REFLECTION

St. Paul writes, "The world itself will be freed from its slavery to corruption" (Rom 8:21). How does the gift of God's Wisdom liberate the world from the corruption of consumerism?

WORD

"Let the last word be, he is all in all!" (Sir 43:28).

REFLECTION

What would happen if all of the piano's eighty-eight keys were tuned to the same key? Music would disappear. St. Athanasius writes: "Think of a musician tuning his lyre. By his skill he adjusts high notes to low and intermediate notes to the rest. So too, the wisdom of God holds the world like a lyre and joins things in the air to those on earth, and things in the heavens to those in the air, and brings each part into harmony with the whole" (St. Athanasius, bishop).[8]

Wise people know better than to describe God's harmony by their own single note. To be wise means to live at peace with sounds far too many to orchestrate, yet with confidence that all of them harmonize with God's Wisdom.

Peace is disturbed when the masterpiece of God's harmony is measured by our own single sound. "More than this we need not add/ he is all in all" (Sir 43:28).

QUESTION FOR YOUR REFLECTION

E Pluribus Unum (from many, one) is this nation's motto. Why is uniformity a danger both to religion and to a nation's character?

WORD

"We are not justified by our wisdom, intelligence, piety, or by any action of ours, however holy, but by faith, the one means by which God has justified [us] from the beginning" (St. Clement I, pope).[9]

REFLECTION

Evidence of faith's fruitfulness of good works is impeded when conflicts of "faith alone" or "good works alone" are "doing their thing." Wisdom is the gift that sees faith's reason for living according to God's will. When God's will "to bring all things in the heavens and on earth into one under Christ's headship" (Eph 1:10) is also ours, faith enlivens us to bring forth fruits of God's love.

No, "we are not justified by our wisdom, intelligence, piety, or by any action, however holy." Rather, we are justified when God's gift of faith charges us with the zeal to be mediators of God's gifts of love. Like harvesters of fruit from good trees, the truly wise bear the fruit of God's loving works from the sturdy trees of faith.

QUESTION FOR YOUR REFLECTION

Why is faith from the heart's consent more fruitful than faith lodged only in the mind's assent?

Second Week in Ordinary Time

SUNDAY

WORD

"In rendering judgment, do not consider who a person is; give ear to the lowly and to the great alike, fearing no man, for judgment is God's" (Deut 1:17).

REFLECTION

Those who recognize diversity as the substance of unity enjoy God's gift of wisdom. This wisdom bears no fruit in the caste system where harmony, healing, and peace are absent.

Jesus comes not to create a "melting pot" but to respect all human beings for their individual and collective worth in the mind of his Father. We are worth *being* the likeness of God's image! This worth transcends

11

the heights of castes where dwellers seek the approval of their worth from rulers.

St. Ignatius of Antioch longs only for God's approval. For him, that approval involves a lifetime of ascending to the perfection of discipleship. "I am now beginning to be a disciple. . . . I am taking the opportunity to urge you to be united in conformity with the mind of God" (St. Ignatius of Antioch, bishop and martyr).[10]

Those who have the mind of Christ understand his good news: "I no longer speak of you as slaves, for a slave does not know what his master is about. Instead, I call you friends, since I have made known to you all that I heard from my Father." (John 15:15).

QUESTION FOR YOUR REFLECTION

How does wisdom enable us to live peacefully in diversity?

MONDAY

WORD

"When you come together frequently, Satan's powers are undermined, and the destruction that he threatens is done away with in the unanimity of your faith" (St. Ignatius of Antioch, bishop and martyr).[11]

REFLECTION

Eastern Europe's enslaved peoples did not gather with weapons of war to free themselves. They assembled only with the wisdom fifty years of indignity could not extinguish. In the light of wisdom's power they revealed the imperishability of freedom's refusal to be extinguished. They demonstrated that when people gather in peaceful assembly, "the destruction that [Satan] threatens is done away with in the unanimity of . . . faith."

The Church assembles us not because physical presence is salvation's obliging factor. We assemble to remember our created purpose to be the likeness of God's communion of persons. Our Eucharistic assemblies oblige God to make the power of Christ's real presence felt in our assembled presence. In the face of such power, Satan is no match for assembled faith.

QUESTION FOR YOUR REFLECTION

How does the foolishness of "Catholic clout mentality" endanger our ecclesial opportunity of being the embodiment of God's peaceful presence?

TUESDAY

WORD

"*Hear, O Israel! The LORD is our God, the LORD alone!*" (Deut 6:4).

REFLECTION

When a scribe asks Jesus, "Which is the first of all the command-ments?" (Mark 12:28), Jesus leads him beyond the mind-set of legalities that scribes held to be the substance of religion. He takes him to "the first" law, indelibly marked on the very nature of all men and women: "Hear, O Israel! The Lord our God is Lord alone!" (Mark 12:29).

With this reply, Jesus justifies all laws. He contends that God, not laws of human craft, defines the code of rightness and wrongness al-leged to be the justification for God's approval. For Jesus, the reason for laws is God's identity, whose only law is the love that compels God to "make man in our image, after our likeness" (Gen 1:26).

Jesus makes it clear that no commandment ranks with God's iden-tity of love. He sees no meaning in a way of life that links righteous-ness to law. If love, then, is God's only law, then the nobility to be God's likeness obliges us to live by two commandments: "You shall love the Lord your God with all your heart, with all your soul, with all your mind, and with all your strength [and] you shall love your neighbor as your-self" (Mark 12:30-31).

QUESTION FOR YOUR REFLECTION

Why did Jesus rank love as the greatest commandment?

WORD

> *"You are a people sacred to the LORD . . . a people peculiarly his own"* (Deut 7:6).

REFLECTION

God's favor is not acquired; we already possess it. "It was not because you are the largest of all nations that the LORD . . . chose you," Moses said, ". . . It was because the LORD loved you and because of his fidelity" (Deut 7:7-8).

We are the recipients of God's love and fidelity because we bear the marks of love's identity. God loves us because "God is love" (1 John 4:8). Jesus comes not only to reveal divine love but also to establish its presence here on earth until the end of time. That presence is his body, the Church.

The Church is the communion of "people sacred to the LORD" graced to be sacraments of God's loving communion of persons. A people conscious of being sacraments of Christ's body will never fail being the likeness of God's communion of love among three persons.

What we offer to God from the fruits of earth's identity does not win God's favor; *who* we are as members of Christ's body places us in the favor of Jesus Christ, whose identity we share. This is the favor of God we already possess.

QUESTION FOR YOUR REFLECTION

What attitude does the phrase "getting more grace" reflect?

WORD

> *"When we speak of Christ's priesthood, what else do we mean than the incarnation?"* (Fulgentius of Ruspe, bishop).[12]

REFLECTION

The flesh of humankind is not a nothing. God envisions it to be the instrument that mediates and reveals the presence of God. That revelation is humanity's glory. It is the ongoing incarnation of God's presence in Christ and the meaning of priesthood. It is the glory of mediating Christ's saving presence in the world. St. Paul grasps the dignity of human life. He writes, "To me, 'life' means Christ" (Phil 1:21), for he "emptied himself and took the form of a slave, being born in the likeness of men" (Phil 2:7). St. Paul sees that in the emptiness to which our first parents were reduced, Christ gives human life the joy of becoming the "royal priesthood" (1 Pet 2:9) that joins heaven and earth.

"It is [in Christ] that our human nature becomes a redemptive offering. When we offer our prayers through him, our priest, we confess that Christ truly possesses the flesh of our race."[13]

QUESTION FOR YOUR REFLECTION

Why does poor self-esteem degrade the incarnation?

FRIDAY

WORD

"No one who is in love with . . . self is capable of loving God" (Diadochus of Photice, bishop).[14]

REFLECTION

Jesus says, "You shall love the Lord your God with your whole heart, with your whole soul, and with all your mind. . . . You shall love your neighbor as yourself (Matt 22:37, 39). Are these words of Jesus and those of Diadochus inconsistent?

Love of self and self-indulgence are not the same. Those who love God with the *wholeness* of selfhood have obviously discovered that human life stands beyond perishables that glory in ego indulgence.

A love of self that concentrates only on the pursuit of indulgence is a love that addicts its pursuers to highs of momentary pleasure that blind them to the love that longs to raise creatures of God's image to the heights where that image dwells. True love of self opens such lovers to the beauty and goodness of this destiny. They marvel at their humanity raised to the dignity of being Christ's incarnation.

We love our selfhood when we experience the joy of being wholly loved by God. "The measure of [our] love for God," writes Diadochus, "depends upon how deeply aware [we] are of God's love for [us]."[15] Without that awareness, love of self is merely self-indulgence.

QUESTION FOR YOUR REFLECTION

Why is self-indulgence the product of poor self-esteem?

SATURDAY

WORD

> *"No one shall appear before the LORD empty-handed"*
> (Deut 16:16).

REFLECTION

The paschal mystery is not solely reserved to Jesus Christ. Nor is it reserved to ritual remembrance confining worshipers to enclaves of ritual performance. The passion, death, and resurrection of Jesus takes place in our humanity so that this mystery might be the property of all.

To be mere spectators of Christ's paschal mystery and its daily Eucharistic remembrance is to "appear before the Lord empty-handed." At the throne of God's judgment no oblation is more pleasing to God than those whose earthly lives give evidence of the paschal mystery's fruitfulness, likeness to Jesus Christ. "The oblation of the Church which the Lord taught was to be offered throughout the whole world, has been regarded by God as a pure sacrifice, and is acceptable to [God]" (St. Iranaeus, bishop).[16]

The Church's Ordinary Time exhorts us to become what we celebrate. The marvels of Christ's paschal mystery unfold in ordinary lives free of sin. Ordinary people become likenesses of Christ, who was raised with all of humanity to an eternity of peace.

QUESTION FOR YOUR REFLECTION

Someone said, "Beware of liturgy that has become lethargy!" Why do some say, "I get nothing out of going to Mass"?

Third Week in Ordinary Time

SUNDAY

WORD

"On Sunday the Christian faithful ought to gather together, so that by listening to the word of God and sharing the Eucharist they may recall the passion, death and resurrection of the Lord Jesus." (Constitution on Sacred Liturgy, 7-8).[17]

REFLECTION

"From age to age you gather a people to yourself, so that from east to west a perfect offering may be made to the glory of your name" (Eucharistic Prayer III).[18]

These words define the Church. It is the universal gathering of all baptized men and women called to be living sacraments of Christ's paschal mystery, his "passion, death and resurrection." This Eucharistic gathering is commissioned to be "a perfect offering . . . made to the glory of [Christ's] name."

The Eucharist bestows the nobility that obliges gathering. It springs from humankind's purpose. The Eucharistic gathering is a sacrament of God's communion of three persons, the communion that God decrees to be the identity of all men and women. This is the nobility that obliges universal gathering.

The Church is not the gathering of saints; it is the gathering of sinners called to be saints. The Eucharist is not ritual obligating mere physical gathering. It is a way of life whose Word attracts sinners to see

17

hope in the lives of sinners longing for the communion of saints. The nobility of this hope obliges both saints and sinners to share "the" perfect offering . . . made to the glory of [Christ's] name."

QUESTION FOR YOUR REFLECTION

Why is Eucharistic gathering obligatory?

MONDAY

WORD

"Husband and wife, by the covenant of marriage, are no longer two, but one flesh" (Pastoral Constitution on the Church in the Modern World, 48).[19]

REFLECTION

It has not gone unnoticed that God is faithful even when confronted with persistent unfaithfulness. God's faithfulness is called "covenant."

Long before Christ's coming, repeated repentance by God's people gave evidence that they cherished the nobility of being wedded to the covenant. This covenant identifies humankind's capacity for its like.

All men and women have been awed by those whose love and fidelity have been consistent with their words about love and fidelity. This consistency is the image of God and is the reason why the Church has elevated matrimony to the dignity of a sacramentality that reveals God's permanence of love. It celebrates the permanence of two people's commitment to be sacraments of God's identity: "God is love" (1 John 4:8).

QUESTION FOR YOUR REFLECTION

The sacrament of matrimony asks for permanence of commitment. How does this requirement act as a sign of God's covenant?

WORD

"You shall take some first fruits of . . . the soil which you harvest from the land . . . and . . . go the place which the Lord, your God, chooses for the dwelling place of his name" (Deut 26:2).

REFLECTION

When Moses speaks to his people about their reentry into the land God promised as their heritage, he obliges them to acknowledge their responsibility of espousal to God's faithfulness. Moses requires his people to offer the "firstfruits" of their harvest so that its "firstfruits" might mirror God's penchant to give only the best.

God does not need harvest's "firstfruits." God asks only for evidences of God-like faithfulness. These evidences echo Christ's fidelity of commitment, whereby humanity becomes the "firstfruits" of God's identity. Such commitment is the glory of Christ and the substance of a happy marriage between heaven and earth.

"[Christ] is so good that he asks no recompense except our love: that is the only payment he desires. To confess my personal feelings when I reflect on all these blessings I am overcome by a kind of dread and numbness at the very possibility of ceasing to love God." (St. Basil the Great, bishop).[20]

QUESTION FOR YOUR REFLECTION

Jesus Christ is God's offering of heaven's "firstfruits" to us. What is ours?

WORD

"Where can the weak find a place of firm security and peace, except in the wounds of the savior?" (St. Bernard, abbot).[21]

REFLECTION

Each person does not carry his or her own cross. There is only one cross. It is the cross that claimed the human life of Jesus and all who claim him as Savior. "In my own flesh," writes St. Paul, "I fill up what is lacking in the sufferings of Christ for the sake of his body, the church" (Col 1:24).

The Church is the body of Christ, who is its head. Just as the head shares the pain of each member, so Christ shares the pain of all. Jesus links himself to each person's suffering so that his presence might transform pain into the credential for communion with God. Christ offers his saving wounds to the members of his body so that they might offer their wounds as the prime condition for reconciliation with God, neighbor, self, and creation.

How tragic to consider sufferings as signs of God's displeasure! Quite to the contrary, sufferings entitle us to intimacy with Christ, whose suffering we complete. This intimacy moves us to proclaim the Eucharist's joyful acclamation, "When we eat this bread and drink this cup, we proclaim your death, Lord Jesus, until you come in glory" (Memorial Acclamation).[22]

QUESTION FOR YOUR REFLECTION

At no time are we closer to Jesus than in time of suffering. Why?

THURSDAY

WORD

" 'The Lord is my light and my salvation; whom shall I fear?' How great was that servant who knew how he was given light, whence it came, and what sort of [person] was formed by that light" (John the Serene, bishop).[23]

REFLECTION

The light of Christ is not for the eyes; it is light for the heart. "What other light," asks John the Serene, "did [Jesus] mean but himself, so that those who have eyes may not see [yet] the blind may receive 'the light.'?"[24]

If, then, the light of Christ is the presence of Christ in our midst, what do we see that the blind can also see? We see the Church's mission of reconciliation taking place. This mission seeks to gather all men and women into the likeness of God's communion. It is in this communion that the light of God's Sun of Justice "with . . . healing rays" (Mal 3:20) illumines hearts and fills them with joy.

"The Church is grounded in the great event of reconciliation between God and humanity which occurs in Christ. The continuation of that ministry is a *constitutive* element of the Church" (italics mine) (NCCB Pastoral and Practice Committee).[25]

The sacrament of reconciliation is indispensable. When we celebrate its forgiveness regularly and frequently, we become instruments of Christ's light showing hostages of sin the way to the communion of saints. Indeed, "how great was that servant who knew how he was given light, whence it came, and what sort of [person] was formed by that light."

QUESTION FOR YOUR REFLECTION

If Christ the Light is already in the world, why is the sacrament of reconciliation a necessity?

FRIDAY

WORD

"The LORD has told me that I shall not cross this Jordan. It is the LORD, your God, who will cross before you." (Deut 31:2-3).

REFLECTION

The note of sadness near the end of Deuteronomy becomes, in Christ, a song of joyful gratitude. Moses' failure to reach the goal of forty years of desert pilgrimage serves to highlight everyone's access to Christ's passover into eternal life.

Death denied Moses access to Jordan's waters. But the death and resurrection of Jesus grants humankind access to the waters of baptism. Jesus' name, "Savior," represents his saving death enabling all to pass over from eternal death to eternal life. Prophetically Moses exclaims: "It is the LORD, your God, who will cross before you." How significant that the task of leading God's people across the Jordan went to Joshua, whose name means "the Lord is salvation." Joshua became the central figure in Israel's history of passover pilgrimage, leading God's people into a land of freedom, security, and peace. In like manner, Jesus is humanity's passover to salvation. All who follow him through suffering's desert experience proclaim gratefully and joyfully: "The Lord is salvation."

QUESTION FOR YOUR REFLECTION

How does St. Paul's frequently used expression "in Christ" relate to the passover experience?

SATURDAY

WORD

"[Humanity] carries within [itself] the seed of eternity"
(Pastoral Constitution on the Church in the Modern World).[26]

REFLECTION

The sadness of our temporary tenure in the world is offset by the belief that "the seed of eternity" lies within us. This seed requires only the patient acceptance of daily dyings, which allows the kingdom to bear fruit within us.

Heaven is not deferred happiness. It is a happiness that, in Christ, can be experienced by the joyful longings that dismiss death's appearance of life's demise. Life's temporary tenure on earth is the daily journey of those who follow Christ's way from sin to sanctity and his pilgrimage from death to resurrection.

The reason we fear death is not because we disbelieve heaven's existence; it is because we don't want to die. Fear of death is an unmistakable signal that along with faith in heaven's existence we must likewise believe that Christ's "way" of the cross is the way for disciples to arrival there.

Within each of us is the "seed of eternity." For it to bear the fruit of eternal life, it must die. "I solemnly assure you," Jesus asserts, "unless the grain of wheat falls to the earth and dies, it remains just a grain of wheat. But if it dies, it produces much fruit" (John 12:24).

QUESTION FOR YOUR REFLECTION

If the "seed of eternity" is already within us, why is there a felt fear of suffering and death? *Jan 30. 2005*

Fourth Week in Ordinary Time

SUNDAY

WORD

"Our preaching of the gospel proved not a mere matter of words for you but one of power" (1 Thess 1:5).

REFLECTION

The gospel is not a collection of words about Christ; it is the power and presence of Christ preached in the witness of our humanity. The gospel is substance for sanctity.

The power of God's Word convinces when it springs from the hearts of Christians. "The first means of evangelization," asserts Pope Paul VI, "is the witness of an authentically Christian life."[27] When home for God's Word is the mind, it bears the fruit of words. When home for God's Word is the heart, it bears the fruit of "an authentically Christian life."

St. Paul's and Pope Paul VI's views on evangelization link two thousand years of Catholic mission. Their views are not addressed to elite corps of preachers. They are addressed to all who *wholeheartedly* listen to and act on the power of God's ever present Word. Both St. Paul and Pope Paul VI praise the eloquence of Christians' authentic witness as the most effective instrument of evangelization.

QUESTION FOR YOUR REFLECTION

Why did Pope Paul rank "witness" as the companion of preaching?

MONDAY

WORD

"It is good and pleasant for brothers [and sisters] to dwell in unity, because when they do so their association creates the assembly of the Church" (St. Hilary of Poitiers, bishop).[28]

REFLECTION

"Behold," sings the psalmist, "how good it is, and how pleasant,/ where brethren dwell as one!/ It is as when the precious ointment upon the head runs down . . ." (Ps 133:1).

Anointment has been the common practice of both Jews and Christians. Oil is the symbol of healing and the unity that healing restores. The Catholic Church's sacramental use of oil symbolizes its awareness of the Church's mission to heal divisions defacing ecclesial identity.

The Church clearly states its identity: "By her relationship with Christ, the Church is a kind of sacrament or sign of intimate union with God, and of the unity of all [humankind]. She is also an instrument for the achievement of such [communion]."[29]

The Church defines both its identity and its mission. It has been anointed not only to be the witness of communion but also the "instrument for the achievement" of that mission. The Church untiringly endeavors to be the witness of Christ's prayer: "I pray . . . that all may be one . . . that the world may believe that you sent me" (John 17:20-21).

QUESTION FOR YOUR REFLECTION

Why is oil used for baptism, confirmation, holy orders, and the sacrament of the sick?

WORD

"We beg you and exhort you In the Lord Jesus . . . to make still greater progress" (1 Thess 4:1).

REFLECTION

Christians who believe that no "greater progress" in holiness is possible in their lives face a bridgeless ravine between themselves and God. The assumption that holiness can be fully attained in this world reveals a twofold arrogance.

First, there is the illusion that one has reached perfect holiness. This fosters the conviction that life on earth enjoys sovereignty with God. To crown oneself with perfection is to become a master of pride, a word with "I" at its center. Because "I" is vertical, bridges can never be built over ravines that separate the prideful from the prayerful.

Second, those who see no need for "greater progress" arrogantly deny humanity's limitless capacity for communion with God. Though we are all born into a world of mortality, we are created for communion with God's immortality. "How else," writes St. Iranaeus, "could this union have been achieved if we had not first become what we are?" (St. Iranaeus, bishop).[30] This becoming requires "greater progress."

QUESTION FOR YOUR REFLECTION

How are denials of "greater progress" the mind-set that advocates euthanasia?

WEDNESDAY

WORD

"The light of true knowledge [shows us] the path of justice, leads us to the Sun of Justice [who] brings the mind into the limitless light of knowledge" (Diadochus of Photice, bishop).[31]

REFLECTION

The sun shines from afar to shed light on the near. The Son of God was sent from afar that we might discern by his light the path of justice in our midst.

The prophet Malachi writes: "For you who fear my name, there will arise/ the sun of justice with its healing rays" (Mal 3:20). Long after this prophecy, the Son of God came into the world as the Sun of Justice, "the light of true knowledge" for humankind's pilgrimage on "the path of justice."

The light of God's "Sun" enables us to distinguish between what is and what is not the will of God. This is discernment, a gift that never fails when human life is open to the light of Jesus directing us on the "path of justice."

How is discernment nourished? "Maintain great stillness," answers Diadochus of Photice, "even in the midst of struggles. We shall then be able to distinguish between different types of thoughts that come to us: those that are good, those sent by God, we shall treasure in our memory; those that are evil . . . we shall reject."[32]

QUESTION FOR YOUR REFLECTION

Discernment is God's gift. Why is the prayer of "stillness" necessary for the effectiveness of this gift?

THURSDAY

WORD

"You endure these as an expression of God's just judgment, in order to be found worthy of his kingdom" (2 Thess 1:4-5).

REFLECTION

The first purpose of judgment is revelation, not condemnation. Judgment arises from the discernment that reveals who we *really* are and who we have been called to be. This revelation from the "Sun of Justice" appears when faithfulness to integrity resists persecution and trial.

Integrity's resistance is also the judgment that condemns injustice by the light of God's Son. Those who resist this light become allied with the injustice that warrants condemnation. "He 'will inflict punishment on those who do not acknowledge God nor heed' the good news of our Lord Jesus Christ" (2 Thess 1:8). St. Paul's words are severely merciful. When discerned as the opportunity for repentance they open the path of repentance leading to justice for all who "acknowledge God" and, "heed the good news of our Lord Jesus Christ." This is the path to peace, freedom, and security that God has promised, a promise kept when respect for human life and its dignity is ablaze in us from God's "Sun of Justice."

QUESTION FOR YOUR REFLECTION

We are created in the likeness of God. What, then, is the basis for God's justice?

FRIDAY

WORD

"In . . . varied ways does grace work within [us] and many are the means by which it leads the soul."[33]

REFLECTION

"I found it!" This was the "good news" of a movement of the early 1970s that quickly evaporated. It evaporated because its decree-like finality was inconsistent with mystery's longing to be revealed. "I found it" failed to find its way into hearts filled with questions to which mystery never ceases to give birth.

A fourth-century homilist cautions against declaring final earth's times of joy and exaltation. We live lives, he insists, of tension between joy and grief, exaltation and lowliness, war and peace, success and failure. It is in those "varied ways" that God's grace works within us, for "many are the means by which it leads the soul."

Many people unexpectedly find the joy of God's presence in their sorrows. Sorrows exist simply because God longs to raise everyone to

27

joys yet to be found. "We pray," speaks the fourth-century homilist, "that we [may be led] . . . into the fullness of divine will and [that God] will refresh us with the varied kinds of his repose, that by the help of this guidance . . . we may be considered worthy to attain to the perfection of the fullness of Christ."[34]

QUESTION FOR YOUR REFLECTION

Sorrow is one of grace's "varied ways" to spiritual growth. What is one sorrow in your life that became a marvelous grace?

SATURDAY

WORD

"May the Lord rule your hearts in the love of God and the constancy of Christ" (2 Thess 3:5).

REFLECTION

When people ask, "What are you worth?" they hardly expect the answer, "I am worth likeness to God's image." That worth is far more than what we possess. Such is not the mind of cultures that measure success by earthly possessions.

Christ's rule measures rather than dominates. God's Son came into the world as love's identity, making visible the measure God has of human worth. When Christ became human, all of humanity became the symbol by which men and women can measure their worth.

Symbols are not conversation pieces expressing nostalgia's rule over our hearts. Symbols are instruments by which we express Christ's rule *in* our hearts. This rule of Christ the King measures both human worth and its capacity to love what lies beyond this world's possessions. Our worth frees "the Lord [to] rule [our] hearts in the love of God and the constancy of Christ."

What are we worth? We are worth the death of Christ on the cross and our destiny to share his resurrection forever. Nothing of this world's worth can buy that!

QUESTION FOR YOUR REFLECTION

How is success measured by earthly possessions destructive of human dignity?

Fifth Week in Ordinary Time

SUNDAY

WORD

> *"God has given a just law to unjust [humanity] in order to show them their sin, not to take it away"* (St. Augustine, bishop).[35]

REFLECTION

Road Closed. Follow Detour.

Signs like this direct travelers to their destination by a roundabout way.

Following his conversion St. Paul discerns that the law had for him been a detour and that Christ has come to be salvation's "way." He warns the Galatians about alleged Christians whose faith in the law keeps open the detour around the saving presence of Christ. "I assure you, . . . the gospel I proclaimed to you is no mere human invention. I did not receive it from any man, nor was I schooled in it. It came by revelation from Jesus Christ" (Gal 1:11-12).

The abolition of law is not St. Paul's issue. Nor is it the issue of Jesus, who says, "Do not think that I have come to abolish the law and the prophets. I have come, not to abolish them, but to fulfill them" (Matt 5:17). For both Christ and St. Paul law is fulfilled when it exposes the dangers to Christ's centrality in our lives. Jesus Christ is human life's fulfillment—"the way, and the truth, and the life" (John 14:6).

The Epistle to the Galatians remains current. It continues to warn of spurious spiritualities that enthrone law as the ultimate way to salvation. Jesus Christ rather than law, St. Paul insists, is the way to salvation. Laws that become the heart of Christian spirituality transform detours into roads closed.

QUESTION FOR YOUR REFLECTION

What is the necessity for religion's laws? What are their limitations?

MONDAY

WORD

"Through the Holy Spirit . . . we receive the gift of faith 'and through faith Christ lives in our hearts' " (St. Bonaventure, bishop).[36]

REFLECTION

St. Paul's encounter with Christ on the way to Damascus is not ordinary. Christ's ordinary way is encounter with him through the gift of faith that testifies, "Christ lives in our hearts." This faith nourishes understanding of the Scriptures, which possess the power of transforming us into the likeness of Christ.

After his ascension Jesus sent the Holy Spirit to form disciples into the embodiment of his abiding presence. This embodiment is the Church. To believe that Christ is encountered in his Church is normative. It is in Christ's ecclesial presence that the light of God's Word is ignited from the gift of faith.

Christians must never ignore the relationship of Church and Scripture. When they divorce Scripture from the Church's ongoing maternity of Christ's presence, they create divisions that also divorce faith's light from Scripture. These divisions hide the truth behind caricatures that mask its beauty. Christianity is fully alive when ecclesial faith leads us to encounter deeper understandings of God's Word." "Faith," writes St. Bonaventure, "is the foundation of the whole Bible, a lamp and key to its understanding."[37]

QUESTION FOR YOUR REFLECTION

Why does religion's vertical dimension (God and I) divorced from its horizontal dimension (the Church and I) lead to divisions?

WORD

"I have been crucified with Christ, and the life I live now is not my own; Christ is living in me" (Gal 2:19-20).

REFLECTION

The Christian perspective for salvation necessarily includes crucifixion. When this constitutive mark of discipleship is absent, Christian identity is fictitious. "May I never boast of anything," St. Paul declares, "but the cross of our Lord Jesus Christ" (Gal 6:14).

What is the evidence of the crucifixion expected of Christians? It is the tension of integrity demanding consistency of words and actions. This is the tension of discipleship. Christians must live *in* the world but not *of* it. Disciples must live in the world but also in Christ and of Christ.

St. Paul does not hedge. "I still live my human life, but it is a life of faith in the Son of God, who loved me and gave himself for me. I will not treat God's gracious gift as pointless. If justice is available through the law, then Christ died to no purpose!" (Gal 2:20-21).

Through faith's encounter with Christ, who "gave himself for me," St. Paul found "pointless" his encounter with religion's justification of law as the way to salvation. He found "pointless" the crucifixion of giving himself to the letter of the law while ignoring the Spirit of Christ within him. "Now," he writes to the Romans, "we have been released from the law—for we have died to what bound us—and we serve in the new spirit, not the antiquated letter" (Rom 7:6).

QUESTION FOR YOUR REFLECTION

What is the crucifixion that integrity demands?

WORD

"If the law that was given was such that it could impart life, then justice would be a consequence of the law" (Gal 3:21).

REFLECTION

Instinctively we ask in the face of injustice, "How can this be justified?" I say "instinctively" because justice is basic to human nature. Its inborn presence demands the freedom that allows human life the peace of realizing its purpose of growing "steadily in wisdom and age and grace before God and men" (Luke 2:52).

Law is not the identity of justice. Justice looks beyond the mere keeping of law to human life's ultimate meaning. When Moses asks God to give his name from the burning bush, God responds: "I am who am" (Exod 3:14). By this name God proclaims humanity's fullest meaning. "I am who am" is both God's name and God's justifying reason for human existence. Each person's "I am" is justified by his or her sharing in God's image. The freedom to attain that image is justice.

Our link to this justification for human existence is faith, not law. "Before faith came," St. Paul writes, "we were under the constraint of the law, locked in until the faith that was coming should be revealed. . . . The law was our monitor until Christ came to bring about our justification through faith. But now that faith is here, we are no longer in the monitor's charge. Each one of you is a son of God because of your faith in Christ Jesus" (Gal 3:23-26)

QUESTION FOR YOUR REFLECTION

Civil courts reckon justice according to the standard of laws. What is the standard by which God's justice is reckoned?

THURSDAY

WORD

"Now that you have come to know God—or rather, have been known by him—how can you return to those powerless, worthless, natural elements to which you seem willing to enslave yourselves once more?" (Gal 4:9).

REFLECTION

Idolatry contains ominous implications for the psalmist:

. . . idols are silver and gold,
the handiwork of men. . . .
Their makers shall be like them,
everyone that trusts in them (Ps 115:4, 8).

When we surrender our integrity to realities less than the reality destined to be the identity of human integrity, we run the risk of becoming likenesses of lesser gods. We risk addiction.

Addictions force their identity on anyone who surrenders to their lie of freedom. With roots in Eden's garden, this lie continues to decree possession of earthly goods as the reason for human existence as well as the sign of life's success.

When this lie becomes the way, the truth, and the life, freedom becomes the license for exchanging likeness to God into likeness to lesser gods.

Their makers shall be like them,
everyone that trusts them.

QUESTION FOR YOUR REFLECTION

What is God's vision of humanity's freedom?

FRIDAY

WORD

"The flesh lusts against the spirit and the spirit against the flesh; the two are directly opposed" (Gal 5:17).

REFLECTION

"The flesh" means much more than violations of human sexuality. For St. Paul, it represents the perversion of ordaining earthly goods as the ultimate goodness worth everyone's wholehearted pursuit. This perversion gives to what is partial the dignity of being what is whole. To live by this spirit is to live in "the flesh." This solitary confinement destroys the wholeness—the integrity—of body and soul.

33

"Use creatures as they should be used," writes St. Leo the Great, "[and give] praise and glory to their Creator for all that you find beautiful and wonderful in them. See with your bodily eyes the light that shines on earth, but embrace with your whole soul and all your affections 'the one true light which enlightens every[one] who comes into the world'" (St. Leo the Great, pope).[38]

QUESTION FOR YOUR REFLECTION

In what way is living in "the flesh" a form of solitary confinement?

SATURDAY

WORD

"May I never boast of anything but the cross of our Lord Jesus Christ!" (Gal 6:14).

REFLECTION

Wisdom enables us to see that the "cross of our Lord Jesus Christ" and ours are one. We boast of Christ's cross because our sufferings, linked to it, allow Christ's healing work access to all who long to be touched by it.

Joy in linkage to the cross of Christ is the sign of spiritual maturity. Jesus does not expect anyone to suffer alone. We are members of his body, and in that communion we are one with Christ and one with one another. This wholeness is holiness, the perfection of maturity!

Those who live in this communion are wholly accessible to the power of the paschal mystery. We "boast" of our sufferings linked to Christ's cross, certain that this communion leads us to Christ's resurrection. In short, we pass over into God's identity, whose communion is the destiny that justifies human suffering.

QUESTION FOR YOUR REFLECTION

Why are daily sufferings signs of Christ's words, "Come follow me"?

34

Sixth Week in Ordinary Time

WORD

"Be thankful then for what you have received, and do not be saddened at all that such an abundance still remains" (St. Ephrem, deacon).[39]

REFLECTION

Wisdom glows from the humble conviction that one doesn't know everything. To live otherwise is to be imprisoned in the solitary confinement of self-sufficiency.

St. Paul admonishes the Romans: "Do not be wise in your own estimation" (Rom 12:16). And to the Corinthians: "If any one of you thinks he is wise in a worldly way, he had better become a fool. In that way he will really be wise, for the wisdom of this world is absurdity with God" (1 Cor 3:18-19).

Wisdom flows from God when companionship with Christ's sufferings becomes a way of life. When that way appears to some as foolishness, the humble wisely acknowledge that "Christ is everything in all of you" (Col 3:11). Wisdom flows from humility's desire that "primacy may be his in everything" (Col 1:18).

QUESTION FOR YOUR REFLECTION

"The beginning of wisdom is the fear of the LORD" (Prov 9:10). Why is humility rather than terror the substance of "fear of the LORD"?

WORD

" 'Happy is the [one] who has found wisdom.' Even more happy is the [one] who 'lives in wisdom' " (St. Bernard, abbot).[40]

REFLECTION

There are few joys that match the wisdom of discovering the grandeur of God in all of creation.

The world is not an evil place. It contains a treasury whose "pearl of great price" is the wisdom that sees the treasury of God's grandeur in creation. The wise see the world's goods not as commodities to be consumed but as sacraments that bless and give to God. It is for creation's sacramentality that the wise sing joyfully the canticle of Daniel:

Bless the Lord, all you works of the Lord,
praise and exalt him, above all forever (Dan 3:57).

The world's goods, of themselves, cannot link us to God. It is wisdom that enables human minds and hearts to work in creation's vineyard of sacramentality, gently cultivating a harvest of God's beauty. "Let us work in the vineyard of the Lord. . . . Let us work in it and dig up wisdom, its hidden treasure, a treasure we all look for and want to obtain."[41] Wisdom is the harvest that links us to God.

QUESTION FOR YOUR REFLECTION

How is reverence for creation a sign of wisdom?

WORD

"Does not Wisdom call,
and Understanding raise her voice?" (Prov 8:1).

REFLECTION

Wisdom is not merely one of God's possessions. Wisdom is God's identity echoing in humankind's likeness to God proclaiming the reason for human existence. That likeness gives to humanity the dignity of enfleshing Wisdom so that her call might be understood in the raised voices of all men and women. In Christ's divinity, Wisdom calls; in Christ's humanity, Understanding raises her voice in reply.

Wisdom calls us to be sacraments of God's image in daily life. Such witness paves the way for "Understanding [to] raise her voice." Wisdom flows from God's Word within us so that the joy of understanding might break out in praise and blessing.

St. Athanasius writes: "As the word we speak is an image of the Word who is God's Son, so also is the wisdom implanted in us an image of the Wisdom who is God's Son. It gives us the ability to know and understand and so makes us capable of receiving him who is all-creative" (St. Athanasius, bishop).[42]

QUESTION FOR YOUR REFLECTION

Why is understanding a sign that we have heard the call of Wisdom and possess the desire to carry it out?

WEDNESDAY

WORD

*"Wisdom has built her house,
she has set up her seven columns"* (Prov 9:1).

REFLECTION

While on earth, people of faith must live as if in two different houses. One has timely needs, the other, eternal. Both beg for attention. The needs of time beg attention through the hungers and thirsts of the body; the needs of God's timeless house are felt by the presence of "Wisdom [who] has built her house."

In this world's "house," we meet the "house" built by Wisdom. It is a house whose needs are nourished from the "seven columns" of Wisdom's strength: wisdom, understanding, knowledge, counsel, piety, fortitude, and fear of the Lord. With these seven pillars we bridge the houses of both time and timelessness. It is from her "house" that Wisdom calls:

Let whoever is simple turn in here; . . .
Come, eat of my food,
  and drink of the wine I have mixed!
Forsake foolishness that you may live;
  advance in the way of understanding (Prov 9:4-6).

QUESTION FOR YOUR REFLECTION

How is the Church a sacrament of the "house" that "Wisdom has built"?

THURSDAY

WORD

"When we are speaking about wisdom, we are speaking about Christ" (St. Ambrose, bishop).[43]

REFLECTION

A house becomes a home when its dwellers love one another!

Wisdom seeks a house where Christ feels at home. She built this world to be his house (see Prov 9:1), but she built the hearts of loving people to be his homes.

These homes are built of love's substance. St. Ambrose specifies the substance of loving hearts fit to be the homes of Christ: "When we speak about virtue, we are speaking of Christ. When we speak about justice, we are speaking of Christ. When we speak about peace, we are speaking of Christ. When we speak about truth and life and redemption, we are speaking of Christ."[44]

Jesus Christ is at home in hearts whose love is made of virtue, justice, peace, truth, and life and redemption. "Let us keep our eyes fixed on Jesus" pleads the sacred writer (Heb 12:2). When eyes are "fixed on Jesus" wisdom is free to build hearts with love's substance. It is within this substance that Christ is at home.

QUESTION FOR YOUR REFLECTION

Why is Church as home the imperative for it to be the sign or sacrament of Christ's presence in the world?

FRIDAY

WORD

"The entire life of a good Christian is in fact an exercise of holy desire. You do not see what you long for, but the very act of desiring prepares you, so that when [God] comes you may see and be utterly satisfied" (St. Augustine, bishop).[45]

REFLECTION

A bird in the hand is worth two in the bush.

This proverb does not apply to our relationship with God. By focusing only on image of God "in the hand" we miss the joyful surprise of encountering God's image of us. Before we meet the God beyond our imagination we must first meet the self that God longs for us to embrace. It is for the unimaginable that God offers us the priceless gift of faith.

"Faith," writes the author of Hebrews, "is confident assurance concerning what we hope for, and conviction about things we do not see" (Heb 11:1). Faith in the "things we do not see" fires the "holy desire" to see God, whose infinite being can never be held "in the hand."

St. Augustine suggests that waiting for God is a greater blessing than one's grasp of God: "By making us wait he increases our desire, which in turn enlarges the capacity of our soul, making it able to receive what is given to us."[46] Mary sings of her capacity to receive Christ:

My being proclaims the greatness of the Lord,
    my spirit finds joy in God my savior,
For he has looked upon his servant in her lowliness (Luke 1:46-48).

QUESTION FOR YOUR REFLECTION

Why is it impossible to grasp fully who God is?

SATURDAY

WORD

"In earlier times God met his people in a covenant of love and fidelity. Now the Savior of mankind, the Bridegroom of the Church, meets husbands and wives in the sacrament of matrimony."[47]

REFLECTION

A symbol is treasured when its reality is lived, remembered, and celebrated. Far from being a token of nostalgia, a symbol re-members both what was and what is.

Matrimony is a sacred symbol signifying the hidden reality of God's irrevocable covenant with humankind. This sacrament symbolizes the irreversible wedding of Christ's union with humanity. The Church, the body of Christ, is the sacrament of that union, remembered again and again in the sacrament of matrimony.

Matrimony is empty when its reality is not grasped. The reality of that sacrament is the visibility of God's faithfulness. This faithfulness unfolds in the lives of couples who make real their vow, "until death do us part."

Here upon earth we are as close to God's covenant as we are to the Church's sacramentality. To make effective the sacraments we celebrate, we need only to enact the reality to which they point. The fidelity of husbands and wives makes visible the covenant of God and humankind.

QUESTION FOR YOUR REFLECTION

Why is the sacrament of matrimony "until death do us part"?

40

Seventh Week in Ordinary Time

WORD

"Nothing is new under the sun" (Eccl 1:9).

REFLECTION

When the Son of God came to dwell "under the sun" he challenged Solomon's "Nothing is new under the sun." He continues to verify God's irrevocable intent: "See, I make all things new!" (Rev 21:5).

Solomon perceives "vanity of vanities" (Eccl 1:2) as purposeless life. His wisdom sees the futility of creation destined only for sense satisfaction:

> The eye is not satisfied with seeing
> nor is the ear filled with hearing (Eccl 1:8).

Jesus came to open the door to a destiny truly new under the Son. The Son of God is the light of God's Wisdom, allowing us to see newness both in ourselves and in all of creation. This is the newness that humankind traded for Eden's tree but that Jesus restored on the tree of his crucifixion. His death and resurrection opens the door for God's love to liberate us from purposelessness "under the sun."

In the light of God's Son, there *is* something "new under the sun."

QUESTION FOR YOUR REFLECTION

Miracles do not violate the laws of nature; they point to newness. How is each human being "a miracle"?

WORD

"I went on to the consideration of wisdom, madness and folly. And I saw that wisdom has the advantage over folly as much as light has the advantage over darkness" (Eccl 2:12-13).

REFLECTION

Once held captive by the darkness of egotism, St. Basil the Great's light was liberated when his sister rebuked him for daily displays of self-importance. Basil was utterly speechless, and his repentance led him away from his own self as Wisdom's source to embrace the source of God's Wisdom, Jesus Christ.

St. Gregory of Nyssa observes, "We shall be blessed with clear vision if we keep our eyes fixed on Christ. . . . St. Paul himself and all who have reached the same heights of sanctity had their eyes fixed on Christ, and so have all who live and move and have their being in him."[48]

Basil's repentance moved his whole being away from the darkness of self-grandiosity to the light of Christ. Because he kept his eyes fixed on Jesus, his life continues to radiate the light of Christ throughout the whole Church. St. Basil as well as all of the saints have led many "to the consideration of wisdom, madness and folly," and with "eyes fixed on Christ," they see "that wisdom has the advantage over folly as much as light has the advantage over darkness."

QUESTION FOR YOUR REFLECTION

What is the problem of those who regard saints as fools?

WORD

"There is an appointed time for everything . . . a time to be born, and a time to die" (Eccl 3:1-2).

REFLECTION

Clocks set only by each other are divorced from the sun that sets time. Clocks that tell the time of each other guide all who seek their guidance into purposelessness.

Time is appointed by God, who is timeless. When the time of human purpose is set by God's reason for human existence, we "live and move and have our being" (Acts 17:28) in the light of God's timeless purpose.

God does not set the clock of eternity by the clocks of this world. It is by the "Sun of Justice" (see Mal 3:20) that we are led to the kingdom of light. For now, we set the time of our lives by the light of God's Son as we journey in the shadows of time to the lights of eternity's timelessness. Always to face the "Sun of Justice" is to know what time it is.

QUESTION FOR YOUR REFLECTION

What is the irony of setting the time of our lives by this world's standards of measurement?

WEDNESDAY

WORD

"Any man to whom God gives riches and property and grants power to partake of them . . . has a gift from God" (Eccl 5:18).

REFLECTION

In his book *Song of the Bird,* Anthony de Mello tells of a lowly fisherman "lying lazily beside his boat smoking his pipe." A magnate of the fishing industry chastises the fisherman for his inactivity by pointing to his fleet of boats and equipment, which have brought him untold riches.

"What would I do then?" asks the fisherman.

"Then you could sit down and enjoy life," replies the industrialist.

To which the fisherman responds, "What do you think I am doing right now?"[49]

The compulsion for possessions signifies that one has traded their enjoyment for the anxiety of hoarding them. When we enjoy what we possess without fear of their loss, we possess wisdom's invitation to "taste and see how good the LORD is" (Ps 34:9).

QUESTION FOR YOUR REFLECTION

Which of your possessions do you take time to enjoy?

THURSDAY

WORD

"If you search by means of discussions for the God who cannot be defined in words, he 'will depart further from you' than he was before. If you search for him by faith, wisdom will stand where wisdom lives, 'at the gates.' " (St. Columban, abbot).[50]

REFLECTION

At the behest of faith, wisdom meets us "at the gates" where God cannot be comprehended. Strange as it may seem, incomprehensibility is the "picture" of God seen through the prism of faith. Those who seek to define God by definitions that end at the gates of discussions find themselves strangers to God.

St. Columban asserts that "the God we seek is not one who dwells at a distance from us, for we have him present with us, if only we are worthy."[51] "We are worthy" when we calculate human worth not by monuments of this world's success but by measurements that calculate God's purpose for creating us. Except for faith, human worth is incalculable. When the eyes of faith are fixed on Jesus, intimacy with God shows us the worth with which God esteems us. We "stand where wisdom lives."

What are we worth? The eyes of faith takes us into the inner sanctum of God's mystery, where human worth is defined. When we live our vocation of experiencing God's intimacy, "we have him present with us [because] we are worthy."

44

QUESTION FOR YOUR REFLECTION

What are you worth?

WORD

> *"Go, eat your bread with joy and drink your wine with*
> *a merry heart, because it is now that God favors your works"*
> (Eccl 9:7).

REFLECTION

Wisdom is the gift that links God's Word to creatures whose service is the reason for the incarnation of God's Word. Wisdom is at work when God's Word is seen as the grandeur creation longs to reveal. All of God's creatures groan to be sacraments of that grandeur.

A faith nourished only by literal interpretations of Sacred Scripture is barred from wisdom's nurture. The gift of wisdom, like music's overtones, links the sounds of words to the lofty realities whose grandeur fills all of God's creatures. This is the grandeur that wisdom tells.

Does wisdom summon us "back to the basics"? Yes, if "basics" point to the loftier meanings of God's words and creatures. What is both basic and lofty about "Go, eat your bread with joy and drink your wine with a merry heart, because it is now that God favors your works"? St.Gregory of Agrigentum writes, "A spiritual interpretation of [these words] leads to a loftier meaning and teaches us to take this as the heavenly and mystical bread which comes down from heaven, bringing life to the world, and to drink a spiritual wine with a cheerful heart, that wine which flowed from the side of the true vine at the moment of his saving passion."[52]

"Taste and see how good the LORD is" (Ps 34:9). For wisdom, this is basic to the food and drink of both earth and heaven!

45

QUESTION FOR YOUR REFLECTION

The Eucharist's real presence of Christ contains lofty implications for bread and wine. What lofty meaning does the "real presence" imply for human life?

SATURDAY

WORD

"However many years a man may live, let him . . . remember that the days of darkness will be many" (Eccl 11:8).

REFLECTION

"Dad," a small boy remarked, "we don't have enough windows for the sun to ripen all of these green tomatoes!"

His father replied, "Tomatoes grow in the sun but ripen in the darkness."

And so it is with our relationship with Jesus, God's "Sun of Justice." Sent as nourishment for the inner regions of human life, his presence in the darkness of inner selfhood allows followers of Christ to "ripen" into the holiness that radiates the light of God's Son.

"Sunlight," writes St. Gregory of Agrigentum, "is a symbol. What we see with our eyes foretells the coming of the Sun of Justice. . . . It is our supreme delight to behold him and contemplate his divine splendor with the eyes of our spirit. When we [share in] that beauty we are enlightened and adorned . . . with the sweetness of the Spirit, in being clothed in holiness [and] in achieving wisdom. . . . We are filled with a joy that comes from God and endures through all the days of our earthly life. . . . For all who gaze upon the Sun of Justice, he is their supreme delight."[53]

Holiness ripens in the dark nights of the soul!

QUESTION FOR YOUR REFLECTION

St. John of the Cross writes, "On the road to union with God, the night of faith shall guide me."[54] If faith is light, why does St. John of the Cross call it "night"?

Eighth Week in Ordinary Time

WORD

"Naked I came forth from my mother's womb,
and naked shall I go back again.
The LORD gave and the LORD has taken away;
blessed be the name of the LORD!" (Job 1:21).

REFLECTION

A woman dying from cancer begged Mother Teresa of Calcutta to pray that she might have the strength to face death. In her reply Mother Teresa begged permission to pray that she cherish weakness as the strength of her death.

Mother Teresa's reply echoes Job. They suggest that human life is lived between the twin mountains of birth and death. At birth we descend that we might be clothed with the strengths that sustain us for life in this world. At death we are carried to the peak of weakness, where we await being clothed in the strength of eternal life.

Faced with death, we do not need this world's strengths. Rather, we need only to be poor in spirit that we might recognize and embrace the simplicity of God's love, our garment for all eternity. Our nakedness of this world's possessions pales before the joy of being clothed with God. In his weakness "Job did not sin, nor did he say anything disrespectful of God" (Job 1:22).

QUESTION FOR YOUR REFLECTION

In the light of Job's plummet from affluence to misery, how can the ageless question "Why must we suffer?" be answered?

WORD

"We accept good things from God; and should we not accept evil?" (Job 2:10).

REFLECTION

The Book of Job is one of Sacred Scripture's seven books of Wisdom literature. It tells of Job's passover from prosperity to affliction and the wisdom of linking them. This integration moves him to say, "We accept good things from God; and should we not accept evil?"

Job's story confirms that both prosperity and affliction are necessary components of human life's tenure on earth. Aware of this duality, St. Gregory the Great asserts:

> If a man receives God's gifts, but forgets his affliction, he can fall through his own excessive joy. On the other hand, when a man is bruised by the scourges, but is not at all consoled by the thought of the blessings he has been fortunate to receive, he is completely cast down.
>
> Both attitudes must be united so that one may be supported by the other: the memory of the gift can temper the pain of affliction, and the foreboding and fear of the affliction can modify the joy of the gift (St. Gregory the Great, pope).[55]

QUESTION FOR YOUR REFLECTION

What is the gift that links prosperity and affliction?

TUESDAY

WORD

"Perish the day on which I was born,
the night when they said, 'The child is a boy!'
May that day be darkness" (Job 3:3-4).

REFLECTION

Grief is not a sign of infidelity. Grief expels the selfishness that imprisons fidelity and enables God to be more fully revealed to one's own self.

St. Augustine's grief moves him to confess: "O Lord, the depths of [my conscience] lie exposed before your eyes. Could anything remain hidden in me, even though I did not want to confess it to you? In that case I would only be hiding you from myself, not myself from you."[56]

The Book of Job lays the foundations for understanding the beatitude "How blest are the poor in spirit: the reign of God is theirs" (Matt 5:3). Job becomes poor in spirit not when he has lost his prosperity but when grief cleanses him from the perception that prosperity is proof of fidelity. Job's grief lays bare a spirit cleansed of the lie that prosperity is entitlement to God's favor. His cleansed spirit allows him to see his likeness to God's image. No other entitlement is necessary.

QUESTION FOR YOUR REFLECTION

Why is Job's "Perish the day on which I was born" a sign of fidelity?

WEDNESDAY

WORD

"Late have I loved you, O Beauty ever ancient, ever new,
late have I loved you" (St. Augustine, bishop).[57]

REFLECTION

St. Augustine gives the reason for his late love for "Beauty, ever ancient, ever new." He confesses: "You were within me, but I was outside, and it was there that I searched for you. In my unloveliness I plunged into the lovely things which you created. You were with me, but I was not with you."[58]

St. Augustine discovers in desolation that God has never moved away from him. Francis Thompson's confession echoes St. Augustine's:

I fled him, down the nights and down the days;
   I fled him, down the arches of the years;
I fled him, down the labyrinthine ways
    of my own mind; and in the midst of tears
I hid from him . . . ."[59]

Augustine "fled" because his "unloveliness" enticed him to seek loveliness in God's "lovely things" created only for earthly tenure. When graced to discover that things temporary are not things ultimate he finds Beauty in the loveliness of the self whom Beauty created for Beauty's sake.

QUESTION FOR YOUR REFLECTION

Where can you find "Beauty ever ancient, ever new"?

THURSDAY

WORD

"Should not the man of many words be answered,
   or must the garrulous . . . necessarily be right? . . .
Oh, that God would speak" (Job 11:2, 5).

REFLECTION

After listening to his infant brother's cries, a small boy asked his mother, "Will he never be quiet?"

She replied, "His cries are the only way he can tell us of his needs; it's our job to look behind the cries we can't understand to the needs we can."

The mother's wisdom unmasks the self-righteousness of Job's friend, Zophar. He fails to "look behind" Job's cries so that he might discern God's voice speaking in tongues of misery and pain.

Job's cries are prophetic when heard through the ears of wisdom's discernment. They are the language of God's Wisdom enfleshing humanity's suffering in the cries of the poor: "Oh, that God would speak." God does speak in the cries of his crucified Son, whose humanity echoes

Job's "formless wasteland" (Gen 1:2) of poverty seeking peace, the fruit of justice.

QUESTION FOR YOUR REFLECTION

In what way is the plight of America's homeless millions the voice of Christ? What is he saying in their homelessness?

FRIDAY

WORD

"I have become the sport of my neighbors:
'The one whom God answers when he calls upon him,
the just, the perfect man,' is a laughingstock" (Job 12:4).

REFLECTION

Conspicuous by their difference, a university student and an elderly peasant-type gentleman rode together on a train.

Eying his seat companion praying the rosary, the young man sneered, "Surely you jest as you pray this outdated way."

"I love this manner of prayer, don't you?" asked the companion.

Mockingly, the student replied, "Throw out that rosary and learn science!"

His companion responded, "Sir, I find science very difficult."

With an air of condescension, the student asked for the old man's name and address and pompously promised to send him elementary scientific literature.

As they parted, the student read the old man's card. It read: Louis Pasteur, Director of the Institute of Scientific Research, Paris.

The student's mockery unwittingly surfaced this great man's humility. It was from this soil that wisdom was revealed and buffoonery exposed. Job reflects on God's wisdom:

With him are strength and prudence; . . .
He sends counselors away barefoot,
    and of judges he makes fools.

51

He silences the trusted adviser,
and takes discretion from the aged (Job 12:16-20).

Sharing humility's seat, Job and Pasteur share the same identity card: Wisdom.

QUESTION FOR YOUR REFLECTION

The Latin word *humus* (soil) parents the word "humility." Why does wisdom flourish in that soil?

SATURDAY

WORD

"I know that I am in the right.
If anyone can make a case against me,
then I shall be silent and die" (Job 13:18-19).

REFLECTION

"I know that I am in the right." The poor do not accuse Job of arrogant speech, because they understand that faith and poverty are spouses. In this marriage Job understands that truth's rightness flows from God rather than affluence.

Job's friends mock him because they understand poverty as the infallible sign of alienation from God. Their conviction about prosperity's ultimate meaning condemns Job for being deprived and dispossessed.

Job and his friends part when faith and poverty unite in Job's life. This marriage parents the conviction "I know that I am right." In poverty, faith convinces Job of a truth higher than prosperity's claim of human life's ultimate meaning. The marriage of faith and poverty gives Job the child of wisdom.

QUESTION FOR YOUR REFLECTION

Why does the marriage of faith and poverty give birth to the conviction that asserts, "I know that I am in the right"?

Ninth Week in Ordinary Time

WORD

"Whence, then, comes wisdom,
and where is the place of understanding?" (Job 28:20).

REFLECTION

When Pope Paul VI died on August 6, 1979, I immediately recalled my favorite passage from his document on evangelization:

> "Above all the Gospel must be proclaimed by witness. . . . Let us suppose that [Christians] radiate in an altogether simple and un-affected way their . . . hope in something that is not seen and that one would not dare to imagine. Through their wordless witness these Christians stir up irresistible questions in the hearts of those who see how they live: Why are they like this? Why do they live in this way? What or who is it that inspires them? Why are they in our midst? Such a witness is already a silent proclamation of the Good News and a very powerful and effective one.[60]

The gospel is not a body of knowledge about God. It is the power of God's presence seeking to transform lives by inspiring people to ask Job's question, "Whence, then, comes wisdom, and where is the place of understanding?" (Job 28:12). The gospel is alive in people whose marriage of faith and suffering allows wisdom to speak of human life's meaning in the midst of this world's prosperity. Such wisdom "stirs up irresistible questions" leading to evangelization.

QUESTION FOR YOUR REFLECTION

Why must there be suffering? is an "irresistible question" that can lead to evangelization. How?

WORD

"I cry to you, but you do not answer me;
you stand off and look at me" (Job 30:20).

REFLECTION

The irony of Job's "cry" stems from his misdirected anger. He is angry at himself. He scolds God for the death of an identity that perished with his prosperity. God is silent to the Job who was and waits to speak to the Job who is yet-to-be. God who said to Moses, "I am who am" (Exod 3:14), waits only for Job to echo the "I" of God's "am."

Anger changes into light when humility lets it shine on our real selves. Anger enlightens us to the tragedy of creating an identity built on something other than God. In the light of our destiny to be like God, this world's morsel of worth prompts our angry cry, "You stand off and look at me." In truth, God waits for humility's light to raise the irresistible question, Does God see more in me than do I?

If anger directs us to humility's door, we shall find Christ knocking.

QUESTION FOR YOUR REFLECTION

Jesus says, "Why look at the speck in your brother's eye when you miss the plank in your own?" (Matt 7:3). How can this question become the source of "amazing grace"?

WORD

"Oh, that I had one to hear my case,
and that my accuser would write out his indictment"
(Job 31:35).

REFLECTION

Survival is a basic instinct. Within it is the struggle between human life's beauty and its bestial opponent, anger. Before beauty can survive, the beast must be tamed.

Anger presides in human life defined by possessions. When loss threatens, their guardian, anger, prowls about "like a roaring lion looking for someone to devour" (1 Pet 5:8). If possessions are safe, anger is quiet.

"The man who thinks he is quiet," writes St. Dorotheus, "has within him a passion he does not see."[61] When Job's peace poses as his justice, his anger remains quiet. But when prosperity vanishes, anger erupts. "Oh, that I had one to hear my case, and that my accuser would write out his indictment."

Job's anger is his indictment. He stands accused of defining himself by his possessions. In that dark night of disillusionment, God offers him a vision of justice whose survival reaches beyond this world. This justice reveals the beauty of Job's identity in the likeness of God's image. The beauty of Job's life is the story of everyone.

QUESTION FOR YOUR REFLECTION

How might anger at what we deem to be unjust lead us to embrace what God deems to be just?

WEDNESDAY

WORD

"When one practices first and preaches afterwards, one is really teaching with power" (St. Gregory the Great, pope).[62]

REFLECTION

To Teach as Jesus Did is the title of a pastoral message on Catholic education written in 1972 by the National Conference of Catholic Bishops. To teach as Jesus did liberates the power of God's Word to make both catechesis and evangelization effective. Jesus was sent first to be the witness of God's power and then to confirm it by his teaching. He lived what he had come to teach.

However orthodox the verbal formulation of God's Word, it will fall on deaf ears if spoken by lips only. "Doctrine loses credibility," writes

55

St. Gregory the Great, "if conscience tethers the tongue."[63] The Word of God seeks enthronement in hearts rather than on lips. When the formulation of God's Word is tethered to the hearts of catechists and preachers, the words from their lips evangelize.

We are companions of Jesus' orthodoxy when we "teach as Jesus did." His orthodoxy springs from a heart where God's fullest presence is enthroned. From his heart Jesus lives the truth that his lips speak. When that is the basis for our orthodoxy, we "teach as Jesus did."

QUESTION FOR YOUR REFLECTION

The rite of baptism for infants challenges parents to be the "first and best of teachers" for their children's faith. In what way is the pastoral's title, *To Teach as Jesus Did* a method for parents' role in Catholic education?

THURSDAY

WORD

"Since the daybreak or the dawn is changed gradually from darkness into light, the Church . . . is fittingly styled daybreak or dawn" (St. Gregory the Great, pope).[64]

REFLECTION

Ignorance is not necessarily lack of knowledge. It is the arrogance that judges God's light by one's view of that light. It is about this ignorance that God chastises Job:

Who is this that obscures divine plans with words of ignorance? (Job 38:2).

In God's mind the light of this world is darkness compared to the light of God's "divine plans." The Church stands between the darkness of this world's light and the light of God's plans. It is the "daybreak or dawn" for which it seeks understanding.

As a dawning in this world's darkness, the Church announces that we have been rescued from the serpent's plans for eternal damnation. The Church longs to be understood as a communion of sinners on passover's pilgrimage from sin's darkness to light's sanctity. Understood as "daybreak," the Church arouses the repentance of sinners and readies them to pass over from darkness to light.

QUESTION FOR YOUR REFLECTION

Christ was condemned by zealots of orthodoxy for mingling with lepers. Who are today's lepers who seek the dawn of compassion and healing?

FRIDAY

WORD

"I had heard of you by word of mouth, but now my eye has seen you. Therefore I disown what I have said" (Job 42:5-6).

REFLECTION

"Discernment is the mother of all virtues" (Baldwin of Canterbury, bishop).[65] It is God's gift empowering us to distinguish what is of God from what pretends to be of God. It is the inner "eye" of our likeness to God, moving us to pray with Job, "Now my eye has seen you. Therefore I disown what I have said."

Today, undiscerned "virtue" abounds. Undiscerned choice, for example, has led to legalized abortion. With the Constitution as the inner eye of discernment, this nation proclaims the "sanctity" of private choice. With such "sanctity" as a nation's "virtue," danger of losing the gift of distinguishing between truth and pretense is at hand.

The Church stands as the dawn in the darkness of this danger. Its gift of discernment enlightens people to the choice of following Jesus Christ, who says, "I am the way, and the truth, and the life; no one comes to the Father but through me" (John 14:6). Those who make that choice are enlightened to say, "I disown what I have said."

QUESTION FOR YOUR REFLECTION

What needs to be discerned in the "sanctity" of private choice?

WORD

"Christ himself is the way, and therefore he says: 'I am the way.' This certainly is eminently right for 'through him we have access to the Father' " (St. Thomas Aquinas, priest).[66]

REFLECTION

Something is implemented when its external features have been carried out. Something is received when the meaning of its implementation has been assimilated into one's identity. It does not follow that one's life has been changed by the mere fulfillment of a task. G. K. Chesterton once wryly observed that before declaring Christianity a failure, we ought first to try it.

Christianity is tried when Christ's way of living life is integrated into ours. St. Paul writes, "The life I live now is not my own; Christ is living in me" (Gal 2:20). Repeatedly using the phrase "in Christ" in his letters, he discerns that no earthly way of living life matches the "way" of Jesus. For St. Paul, the mere implementation of Christianity is pious charade: "If I speak with human tongues and angelic as well, but do not have love, I am a noisy gong, a clanging cymbal" (1 Cor 13:1). "Therefore, hold fast to Christ. You will not be able to go astray, because he is the way. He who remains with him does not wander in trackless places; he is the right way."[67]

QUESTION FOR YOUR REFLECTION

Although the features of the Second Vatican Council have been implemented, what is your observation about the extent to which its spirit has been "tried"?

Tenth Week in Ordinary Time

WORD

*"If you keep silent about me, I become a word of God;
but if you love me in the flesh, I become a meaningless cry"*
(St. Ignatius of Antioch, bishop and martyr).[68]

REFLECTION

Feats of human glory are meaningless when eternal glory is not their aim. Human life reaches its zenith when the glory of God is witnessed in discipleship to Jesus Christ.

The desire for martyrdom springs from our discernment of human life's meaning. When we see our role to be "a word of God," martyrdom, however witnessed, mirrors our basic desire to be in Christ.

In his letter to the Romans, St. Ignatius of Antioch pleads with them not to love him only "in the flesh." He argues that as long as he remains on earth he cannot be raised by God to become "a word of God." He writes, "It is a fine thing for me to set with the sun, leaving the world and going to God, that I might rise with him."[69]

Not all of us are called to shed our blood. But we are baptismally called to be witnesses of what life "in Christ" means. The vocation to be "in Christ" is witnessed when we die to this world's way and follow the "way" of Jesus Christ. This is the way of becoming "a word of God."

QUESTION FOR YOUR REFLECTION

If Jesus is God's Word, what does St. Ignatius mean by his freedom to become "a word of God"?

WORD

"Above all, be firm and steadfast" (Josh 1:7).

REFLECTION

Greatness is the fruit of steadfastness. A biographer notes the steadfastness of Poland's great statesman and pianist Ignace Jan Paderewski, who "made a most revealing statement to a group of music lovers after one of his concerts. 'If I would neglect to practice one day, I would notice it. If I would fail to practice a week, my critics would notice it. If I would fail to practice for a month, you, my public, would notice it'" (anonymous).

Steadfastness of commitment is evident when words and actions are consistent. St. Ignatius of Antioch writes of this consistency: "You have never begrudged the martyrs their triumph. . . . I am asking you to be consistent with the lessons you teach them. [Likewise] beg for me the courage and endurance not only to speak but also to will what is right, so that I may not only be called a Christian, but prove to be one."[70]

When Jesus died on the cross, he had remained "firm and steadfast." Likewise, when steadfastness to baptismal commitment is our way of living, the appearance of Christ on the face of the Church verifies greatness as the fruit of steadfastness.

QUESTION FOR YOUR REFLECTION

Had Jesus succumbed to the taunt "Come down off that cross" (Matt 27:40), what inconsistency to his resurrection's meaning would have followed?

TUESDAY

WORD

"Do not have Jesus Christ on your lips and the world in your hearts" (St. Ignatius of Antioch, bishop and martyr).[71]

REFLECTION

St. Ignatius warns against two-faced discipleship, which reveals lack of integrity. Such disciples display the inconsistency of speaking Christ but acting otherwise.

There is, however, another inconsistency that contains the seeds of hope for true discipleship. These seeds lie in the soil of one's inward dispositions longing for the freedom to witness the holiness that endows disciples with integrity. One's inward dispositions are held hostage by outward obeisance to forms of political, economic, social, and cultural correctness.

There is, nevertheless, hope. The passover pilgrimage does not begin on lips but in hearts. It is within the hearts of disciples that conversion's pilgrimage puts to flight the outward inanities holding holiness hostage. St. Ignatius of Antioch speaks with his lips what dwells in his heart: "I no longer wish to live, as men [and women] count life."[72]

QUESTION FOR YOUR REFLECTION

Jesus says, "None of those who cry out, 'Lord, Lord,' will enter the kingdom of God but only the one who does the will of my Father in heaven" (Matt 7:21). What, then, is the will of God?

WEDNESDAY

WORD

"When you see the ark of the covenant of the LORD, your God . . . you must also break camp and follow it, that you may know the way to take, for you have not gone over this road before" (Josh 3:3-4).

REFLECTION

In his poem "The Road Not Taken" Robert Frost reflects:

Two roads diverged in a wood, and I—
I took the road less traveled by,
And that has made all the difference.[73]

The words of both Joshua and Frost contain timeless meaning. The "less traveled" road of Christ's way of the cross offers us its saving "difference." Jesus is the "ark of the covenant" leading us through the waters of baptism and across the desert experience of earthly suffering to the homeland of eternal communion with God.

Pilgrimage on this "road less traveled" leads to marvels that have "made all the difference." Origen comments, "You should not be amazed to hear of . . . wonders performed for [people] of the past. The divine word promises much greater and more lofty things for you who have passed through Jordan's stream by the sacrament of baptism."[74]

To travel the "less traveled" road of Christ's way is to *expect* the miracles that we have been created to become.

QUESTION FOR YOUR REFLECTION

Why are beaten paths also dead-end roads?

THURSDAY

WORD

"Once Jericho was surrounded it had to be stormed. . . . The priests merely sounded the trumpets, and the walls of Jericho collapsed" (Origen, priest).[75]

REFLECTION

The walls of pride separating us from God do not collapse from this world's weaponry. They collapse when assembled peoples storm heaven with prayer.

The ancient story of Jericho's walls, which collapsed at the sound of trumpets and shouts, was relived at Berlin's wall. For thirty years it had divided its people and the people of Europe's eastern nations. This wall did not collapse from guns; it collapsed when millions of no-longer fearful people assembled. Their longing for freedom became a trumpet call for the collapse of Berlin's wall.

"Once Jericho was surrounded it had to be stormed." These words strike fear when weapons of war are the reason for encirclement. They are instruments of peace when trumpets of prayer storm the walls that separate humankind from God.

QUESTION FOR YOUR REFLECTION

When a nation calls weapons of war "peacemakers," why is permanent peace jeopardized?

WORD

"The sun halted in the middle of the sky; not for a whole day did it resume its swift course. Never before or since was there a day like this, when the LORD obeyed the voice of a man" (Josh 10:13-14).

REFLECTION

Christ came at the "Day" that links all days. He is the Day because he is God's "Sun of Justice" (see Mal 3:20) removing the darkness that separates us from union with God. "This is the day the LORD has made; let us be glad and rejoice in it" (Ps 118:24).

Those who daily pray the psalms are the voice that halts the "Sun of Justice" "in the middle of the sky." We live in the "Day" of Christ's redemption, as his psalmody links people of all nations in the glory of God's "Sun of Justice." St. Ambrose writes: "In the psalms . . . not only is Jesus born for us, he also undergoes his saving passion in his body, he lies in death, he rises again, he ascends into heaven, he sits at the right hand of the Father."[76]

QUESTION FOR YOUR REFLECTION

There is that time of day when the sun nears the horizon. In what way is Christ's resurrection "the day the LORD has made"?

SATURDAY

WORD

"This stone shall be our witness, for it has heard all the words which the LORD spoke to us" (Josh 24:27).

REFLECTION

The desire to be remembered is often detected by the permanence we give to the monuments we choose for our remembrance. Joshua chose stone.

King David, however, chose a monument that will ever keep his memory alive. To this day, his psalms are evidence that he had welcomed God into his heart. From there the presence of God has sounded in the hearts of all who pray King David's monumental psalmody.

The psalms have never been erased because their substance is from God. They indelibly marked the life of David and do no less for all whose lives are prayerfully formed by them. The psalms become our identity when God's Spirit transforms the substance of our lives into the substance of their praise. Lives marked by the psalms become lasting monuments of the holiness they inspire.

QUESTION FOR YOUR REFLECTION

Why will the psalms outlive every other monument?

Eleventh Week in Ordinary Time

SUNDAY

WORD

"When we pray, our words should be calm, modest and disciplined. . . . For God hears our heart not our voice" (St. Cyprian, bishop and martyr).[77]

REFLECTION

Words are not the substance of prayer, "for God hears our heart not our voice." Prayer is God's presence drawing us to the intimacy that compels hearts to exclaim, "Our Father in heaven, hallowed be your name . . . ." (Matt 6:9).

St. Cyprian suggests that when prayer is "calm, modest and disciplined," it is coming from hearts, not lips. Prayer is calm because the faith that inspires it arranges our lives around the indwelling presence of God.

Prayer is modest because humility spares us the exaggeration of peership with God.

Prayer is disciplined when daily remembrance of God's fidelity inspires our response to God's longing for intimacy.

QUESTION FOR YOUR REFLECTION

A common complaint: "God doesn't hear my prayer!" What's the problem?

MONDAY

WORD

"We do not say, 'My Father, who art in heaven,' nor 'Give me this day my daily bread'" (St. Cyprian, bishop and martyr).[78]

REFLECTION

America's visitor Alexis Tocqueville expressed fears about American individualism. "Each man," he writes, "is forever thrown back on himself alone, and there is danger that he may shut [himself] up in the solitude of his own heart."[79]

This French visitor envisioned a nation of loners with tragic consequences for the communal dimensions of democracy. His observations also apply to a spiritual individualism that runs counter to humankind's communal nature. Spiritual individualism and prayer are not compatible.

Prayer is effective to the extent that pray-ers acknowledge the communal dimension of the Lord's Prayer. St. Cyprian writes, "It is not for [oneself] alone that each person asks to be forgiven, not to be led into temptation or be delivered from evil. Rather, we pray in public as a community, and not for one individual but for all. For the people of God are all one."[80]

QUESTION FOR YOUR REFLECTION

"I don't get anything out of prayer." What's the problem with that complaint?

WORD

> " 'May your name be hallowed.' It is not that we think
> to make God holy by our prayer; rather we are asking God
> that his name may be made holy in us . . . for we have need
> of daily sanctification" (St. Cyprian, bishop and martyr).[81]

REFLECTION

When God calls Gideon to be Israel's liberator, Gideon objects: "Please, my lord, how can I save Israel? My family is the meanest in Manasseh, and I am the most insignificant in my father's house" (Judg 6:15). These words suggest the humility of heart that longs for an identity "hallowed" with the strength of God's holiness.

The Lord's Prayer presumes humility. With humility's spirit we ask that God's name hallow—sanctify—us with the strength of God's presence. It is a daily reminder that the search for holiness is a daily vocation. Like Gideon, the humble of heart acknowledge that they are the "most insignificant" in their Father's house, because without the seal of God's name, unhallowed selves suffer the loneliness of spiritual isolation.

QUESTION FOR YOUR REFLECTION

"He must increase, I must decrease" (John 3:30). How do these words of John the Baptist relate to Christ's, "Hallowed be your name"?

WORD

> "The prayer continues: 'Your kingdom come.' We pray
> that God's kingdom will become present for us in the same
> way that we ask for his name to be hallowed among us"
> (St. Cyprian, bishop and martyr).[82]

REFLECTION

Faith demands that the roots of human identity be planted in the identity of Jesus Christ. It is in Christ that faith allows our humanity the immediacy of God's kingdom and God's will. In Christ, God's kingdom *has come* and God's will *has been done.*

The Lord's Prayer looks beyond horizons familiar to the eye. With faith's vision, we are opened to endless vistas of God's transcendence already in our midst.

God calls Gideon to look beyond the military "common sense" of divisions. "You have too many soldiers with you for me to deliver Midian into their power, lest Israel vaunt itself against me and say, 'My own power brought me the victory'" (Judg 7:2). Gideon's faith allows him to see *now* the coming of God's kingdom and the completion of God's will.

QUESTION FOR YOUR REFLECTION

If God's kingdom has come and God's will has been done, why did Jesus teach us to pray, "Your kingdom come, your will be done"?

THURSDAY

WORD

"We speak of our daily bread, because Christ is the bread of those who touch his body" (St. Cyprian, bishop and martyr).[83]

REFLECTION

The Eucharist becomes a jubilant celebration for all who witness the reality of its sign; those who celebrate on both sides of the altar believe that they are the body of Christ signified by Christ's sacramental presence.

It ought not go unnoticed that the Lord's Prayer begins the Eucharist's Communion rite. Worshipers pray, "Give us today our daily bread" (Matt 6:11). We acknowledge not only our desire for "daily bread," but also that Christ's love be nourishment for all "who hunger and thirst for holiness" (Matt 5:6).

A Eucharistic people are the body of Christ who break the bread of their lives so that, in Christ, they might be the holiness for all whom they touch.

QUESTION FOR YOUR REFLECTION

What is the twofold meaning of "Give us this day our daily bread"?

FRIDAY

WORD

"The Lord answered . . ., 'Although you press me, I will not partake of your food. But if you will, you may offer a holocaust to the LORD' " (Judg 13:16).

REFLECTION

Whenever the value of an object is, in itself, the reason for sacrifice, the value of sacrifice becomes insignificant. What is offered never outweighs the sacrificial motive of those who sacrifice.

Speaking through Isaiah, the Lord asserts, "What care I for the number of your sacrifices? . . . Cease doing evil; learn to do good. Make justice your aim: redress the wronged, hear the orphan's plea, defend the widow" (Isa 1:11, 16-17).

The "holocaust to the LORD" is the offering of self. What we *do* follows from who we *are*. Sacrifices offered by the unrepentant reek of hypocrisy. They mock Jesus, who, on the cross, is both priest and victim. He is the epitome of integrity.

In his prayer, Jesus speaks of integrity when he prays, "Forgive us the wrong we have done as we forgive those who wrong us" (Matt 6:12). "We are made aware," writes St. Cyprian, "that we cannot obtain what we ask regarding our own trespasses unless we do the same for those who trespass against us [for] 'the measure you give will be the measure you get.' "[84]

68

QUESTION FOR YOUR REFLECTION

What is integrity?

SATURDAY

WORD

"Samson cried out to the LORD and said, 'O Lord GOD, remember me! Strengthen, me O God'" (Judg 16:28).

REFLECTION

A dying cancer patient asked Mother Teresa of Calcutta to pray that she might have the strength to face death. Mother Teresa promised to pray, rather, that she have the weakness to die.

Mother Teresa's reply confronts the temptation that prompted Jesus to pray, "Subject us not to the trial but deliver us from the evil one" (Matt 6:13). What trial? Our temptation to believe that this world's strengths are the ultimate ingredients of happiness.

Failures can be graced moments acknowledging that human strengths are inadequate for salvation. The Lord's Prayer begs that we pray with the understanding that in afflictions "the love of God has been poured out in our hearts through the Holy Spirit who has been given to us" (Rom 5:5).

We never pray the Lord's Prayer alone. At each Eucharist people pray for the strength to believe that in weakness the strength of God is found. "I am content with weakness," St. Paul says, "for when I am powerless, it is then that I am strong" (2 Cor 12:10).

QUESTION FOR YOUR REFLECTION

What failure in your life was a moment of grace?

Twelfth Week in Ordinary Time

WORD

"The LORD said, 'There—anoint him, for this is he!'" (1 Sam 16:12).

REFLECTION

Anointed by Samuel, David sings anointment's meaning:

You love justice and hate wickedness;
therefore God, your God, has anointed you
with the oil of gladness above your fellow kings (Ps 45:8).

"Gladness" fills those whose lives make believable the indwelling presence of the Holy Spirit. The Spirit who anointed Jesus likewise anoints humanity with the "gladness" of serving justice above kings and priests. St. Peter gladly tells the early Christians, "You . . . are 'a chosen race, a royal priesthood, a holy nation, a people he claims for his own to proclaim the glorious works' of the One . . ." (1 Pet 2:9).

We are baptized to be servants of justice, a vocation that proclaims "the glorious works of God." Faithfulness to these "works" marks the lives of a priestly people anointed to bring the "gladness" of justice to all who suffer the indignity of injustice.

QUESTION FOR YOUR REFLECTION

What is the sign that one realizes the meaning of anointment?

WORD

"Saul clothed David in his own tunic, pulling a bronze helmet on his head and arming him with a coat of mail" (1 Sam 17:38).

REFLECTION

"I've got to be me." Frank Sinatra crooned these words into the hearts of a generation ready for the disestablishment of conformity.

Similarly, the boy David begs to be himself when, weighted down with King Saul's attire for battle, he asserts: "I cannot go in these, because I have never tried them before" (1 Sam 17:39). He begs, "I've got to be me."

Uniqueness makes each of us indispensable for the completion of Christ's ongoing incarnation. Baptism encourages us to be disestablished from conformity to this world's spirit so that God's Spirit might anoint each one's uniqueness with "the oil of gladness" (Ps 45:8). It is in each person's uniqueness that Christ's incarnation is handed on.

QUESTION FOR YOUR REFLECTION

When individualism and conformity compete, how is "I've got to be me" a blessing? How a danger?

TUESDAY

WORD

"The life of the Christian has three distinguishing aspects: deeds, words and thoughts. . . . We must make sure that all our thoughts, words and deeds are controlled by the divine ideal, the revelation of Christ" (St. Gregory of Nyssa, bishop).[85]

REFLECTION

When asked, "Why is a sin, sin?" a small boy replied, "Because I is in the middle of it."

Jealousy has become the "I" of King Saul. All of his deeds, words, and thoughts are focused only on the death of faithful David. Saul's whole life is out of control because jealousy rages at the center of his life.

"I" at the center of life divides, conquers, and holds hostage "deeds, words, and thoughts." With no room for inflation, the "I" at one's center ruptures the bond that integrates life's "three distinguishing aspects" and instead bears only the fruits of division.

With Christ's way, truth, and life at the center, our lives "are controlled by the divine ideal, the revelation of Christ."

QUESTION FOR YOUR REFLECTION

We remain unreconciled with others because we are unreconciled with ourselves. What causes division with one's own self?

WEDNESDAY

WORD

"And in his love for David, Jonathan renewed his oath to him, because he loved him as his very self" (1 Sam 20:17).

REFLECTION

Blessed Aelred, abbot, observes: "Jonathan . . . took no heed of his royal lineage or his hope of the throne, but allied himself with David the servant and made him his equal in friendship before the Lord."[86]

Acquaintanceships outnumber friendships because too often there is failure to trust the exchange of each other's wholeness. When the trust level is low, the illusion of friendship is high. That illusion keeps alive the lie that defines equality as the right to possess rather than as "friendship before the Lord." Friendship is based not on what people possess but on who they are.

Jonathan possesses the trust level of Jesus Christ, who exchanges the wholeness of divinity for the wholeness of humanity. Jesus opens humanity to a communion between heaven and earth, a communion initiated when heaven entrusted its wholeness in exchange for earth's. This communion is the substance of friendship.

"I call you friends, since I have made known to you all that I heard from my Father" (John 15:15).

QUESTION FOR YOUR REFLECTION

Why are friendships among adults fewer than among children?

WORD

"My soul grows dizzy when it hears the great voice of the Lord saying: "Blessed are the clean of heart, for they shall see God" (St. Gregory of Nyssa, bishop).[87]

REFLECTION

St. Paul is preeminently "clean of heart," because he sees Christ in everything. He writes: "He is before all else that is. In him everything continues in being . . . so that primacy may be his in everything" (Col 1:17-18).

The clean of heart see the sacredness of all things in the light of God's holiness bringing creation to the dizzying heights of God's wholeness. This wholeness is the holiness in whose identity humankind has been created.

"I am who am" (Exod 3:14) is God's name. God's "I" is the "am" of everything. The clean of heart refuse to split reality into the sacred and the secular, the schizophrenia that denies "primacy" to Christ "in everything."

QUESTION FOR YOUR REFLECTION

Poet Gerard Manley Hopkins writes, "The world is charged with the grandeur of God."[88] What do these words say about the alleged division between the sacred and the secular?

WORD

"Surely the Lord does not encourage us to do something impossible to human nature because the magnitude of what he commands is beyond the reach of our human strength" (St. Gregory of Nyssa, bishop).[89]

REFLECTION

I almost rationalized myself away from a great grace. With a crowd of men and women awaiting my retreat reflections, I found myself devastated by a cold. "Surely," I thought, "God does not expect me to meet these people in this weakened condition."

As I prepared to back out, St. Paul's words changed my mind. "I am content with weakness . . . for the sake of Christ; for when I am powerless, it is then that I am strong" (2 Cor 12:10). From that change of mind I experienced the confirmation of St. Paul's assertion.

God's strength is not a reward for service done in weakness. Service done in weakness makes all the more evident the presence of God's strength. We are poor in spirit when from the fabric of our limitations our faith trusts the magnitude of God's strength. Happy are the poor in spirit because "the happiness God promises certainly knows no limitations."[90]

QUESTION FOR YOUR REFLECTION

"The hour has come for the Son of Man to be glorified" (John 12:23). Why did Jesus link crucifixion with glory?

SATURDAY

WORD

"Blessedness does not lie in knowing something about God, but rather in possessing God within oneself" (St. Gregory of Nyssa, bishop).[91]

REFLECTION

A pianist confessed that he couldn't read a note of music.

"Oh!" replied a crestfallen listener, "You really don't know music, do you?"

"Yes, I do know music," retorted the pianist, "but I don't know about it."

The author of *The Imitation of Christ* says that he would rather experience sorrow within himself than know how to define it. The author, echoing "The reign of God is already in your midst" (Luke 17:21) suggests that Jesus is present to make us witnesses of presence, not encyclopedias of theology.

The clean of heart are not those who "get" the presence of Jesus for something they do. The clean of heart realize that God is Immanuel—"God within us." They are blessed to see God not with their eyes but, with the eyes of faith, to taste here on earth heaven's limitless peace and joy.

QUESTION FOR YOUR REFLECTION

How is faith's vision of heaven's inner presence jeopardized when "clean of heart" refers only to matters of sexuality?

Thirteenth Week in Ordinary Time

SUNDAY

WORD

"Saul had driven mediums and fortune-tellers out of the land. . . . Then Saul said to his servants, 'Find me a woman who is a medium, to whom I can go to seek counsel' " (1 Sam 28:3, 7).

REFLECTION

King Saul fails to be authoritative because his words do not match his actions. He lacks authority because he lacks integrity.

In contrast, people are "spell-bound by his teaching, for his words had authority" (Luke 4:32). In Jesus there is consistency between what he says and how he acts. His deeds empower his words and make credible his authority.

The authority of Christians reveals the integrity of Jesus when their way of life shows the consistency of words with actions. Christians leave people "spellbound" by their teaching when *what* they say they believe is *how* they live what they say.

QUESTION FOR YOUR REFLECTION

What Christians have held you "spellbound" by their teaching?

MONDAY

WORD

> *"You are responsible for your own death, for you testified against yourself when you said, 'I dispatched the LORD's anointed'"* (2 Sam 1:16).

REFLECTION

David does not let revenge blind him to King Saul's dignity of being God's anointed one. He regards anointment not as a gesture for empty adulation but as his responsibility to care for God's people.

Anointment links David to Jesus, who begins his public ministry proclaiming, "The Spirit of the Lord is upon me; therefore, he has anointed me" (Luke 4:18). Jesus' anointment by "the Spirit of the Lord" proclaims his lineage with his Father, who said to him, "You are my beloved Son. On you my favor rests" (Mark 1:11).

What the Father speaks, Jesus intends to live. It is for this integrity that we are anointed to live lives consistent with his words and deeds. We are companions of Christ, and in his Spirit we are the "LORD's anointed."

QUESTION FOR YOUR REFLECTION

How does hypocrisy fracture lineage to Jesus Christ?

WORD

" *'This is our glory: the witness of our conscience.'* . . .
*What defense is there save the witness of our own good con-
science?"* (St. Augustine, bishop).[92]

REFLECTION

When good conscience is assaulted, integrity is revealed. Persecution reveals the bad conscience of those for whom injustice is a way
of life.

Acceptance of persecution is not an exercise of masochism. Integrity
acknowledges that *in* persecution lies the strength of God. "He comforts us in all our afflictions," St. Paul writes, "and thus enables us to
comfort those who are in trouble, with the same consolation we have
received from him" (2 Cor 1:4).

David's conscience is his defense. Clothed with faith it enables him
to see beyond Saul's persecutions to the kingly office of God's anointed.
Because he seeks first for God's glory, his kingship makes straight the
way for Christ's kingship and its glory.

QUESTION FOR YOUR REFLECTION

When conscience is perceived as identity, why is integrity a prime
vocation?

WORD

*"My Lord, could you not have included all in one word
by saying, 'Father, give us whatever is good for us'?"* (St.
Teresa of Avila, virgin).[93]

REFLECTION

Jesus carries the cross made of prayers unexamined.

An unexamined prayer comes from the mother of James and John. For them she begs for high places in the kingdom of their own imagination. Having already examined the implications of this mother's prayer, Jesus asks her sons, "Can you drink of the cup I am to drink of?" (Matt 20:22). Their reply, "We can" (Matt 20:22), falls short of the question's implication.

The petition "your kingdom come" (Matt 6:10) becomes effective when the life of Jesus *as our identity* is examined with its implication of transformation. If that implication is intended, then we are ready to accept Christ's "cup" of suffering on the way of perfection.

QUESTION FOR YOUR REFLECTION

If God granted us every one of our petitions, we would live miserable lives. Why?

THURSDAY

WORD

"Then David, girt with a linen apron, came dancing before the LORD with abandon, as he and all the Israelites were bringing up the ark of the LORD with shouts of joy and to the sound of the horn" (2 Sam 6:14-15).

REFLECTION

Ritual and worship are not the same. People ritualize so that ritual's common understandings might pave the way for communion with God's communion of persons both created and uncreated.

Ritual does not quench thirst for God. It directs us to the living waters of God's loving presence. In ritual of dance and song David abandons himself before the presence of God "with shouts of joy," where he finds the fountain of living waters. As David dances, God speaks the peace that "will soar as with eagles' wings" (Isa 40:31). Worship is our ascent with Christ to the throne of God.

Worship is at home with ritual because the joy of heaven seeks a temple of people assembled in the likeness of God's communion of persons. "The house of God is the Church, his marvelous dwelling place, filled with joyful voices giving thanks and praise, filled with all the sounds of festive celebration" (St. Jerome, priest).[94]

QUESTION FOR YOUR REFLECTION

What is the reason for joyless rituals?

FRIDAY

WORD

"Who am I, Lord GOD, and who are the members of my house, that you have brought me to this point?" (2 Sam 7:18).

REFLECTION

At the height of David's earthly glory, humility speaks: "Here I am living in a house of cedar, while the ark of God dwells in a tent!" (2 Sam 7:2).

But God thrusts David into deeper depths of humility. God shows him a "house" begun in a desert, a house built of people's suffering and God's compassion. Humility calls for David's understanding of God's house as a people whom he had been called to shepherd.

Born of Israel's "house," Jesus is sent to be the cornerstone of God's household of faith, the Church. The followers of Christ, God's household of faith, are likewise the household of God's presence.

Struck with a prophetic vision of God's house, David prays: "Great are you Lord GOD! . . . What other nation on earth is there like your people Israel . . .? You have established for yourself your people Israel as yours forever" (2 Sam 7:22-24).

QUESTION FOR YOUR REFLECTION

The Second Vatican Council described the Church as the People of God. Why are Catholics puzzled by this description?

WORD

"The present is a time for the acknowledgment of sin. Acknowledge what you have done, in word or deed, by night or day. Acknowledge your sins at a time of God's favor, and on the day of salvation you will receive the treasures of heaven" (St. Cyril of Jerusalem, bishop).[95]

REFLECTION

David's adultery with Bathsheba and his order to send her husband to certain death reveals a heart more at home with lust than with love for God's presence.

When mind and heart are not one, hypocrisy reigns. God is not at home in those whose lips speak God but whose hearts lust only for earthly treasures. "Remember," Jesus says, "where your treasure is, there your heart is also" (Matt 6:21).

If our hearts are at home only with this world's treasures, God is not at home in us. To say that we are temples of God is inconsistent when lusts inhabit our hearts. Hearts become homes for God when we acknowledge the truth about our lusts. "Acknowledge your sins at a time of God's favor, and on the day of salvation you will receive the treasures of heaven."

QUESTION FOR YOUR REFLECTION

Religion has been defined as "relinking." Why is the sacramental acknowledgment of sins a necessary act of religion?

Fourteenth Week in Ordinary Time

WORD

"A sacrifice to God is a contrite and humble heart" (St. Augustine, bishop)[96]

REFLECTION

David's sins of adultery and murder pale before the magnitude of his repentance. From the depths of his heart he lays bare the sacrifice of a crushed heart. His repentance speaks prophetically of St. Augustine's words centuries later: "You now have the offering you are to make. No need to examine the herd, no need to outfit ships and travel to the most remote provinces in search of incense. Search within your heart for what is pleasing to God. Your heart must be crushed."[97]

The sacrament of reconciliation is effective when the repentance that it celebrates is the deeds of its penitents. It celebrates hearts that are contrite—crushed. It celebrates the peace of all who have acknowledged, "I am a sinner." It celebrates the consolation of Christ's words: "Take my yoke upon your shoulders and learn from me, for I am gentle and humble of heart. Your souls will find rest, for my yoke is easy and my burden light" (Matt 11:29-30).

QUESTION FOR YOUR REFLECTION

"I don't go to confession because I don't get anything out of it." What is faulty about the reasoning of this assertion?

WORD

"The Israelites have transferred their loyalty to Absalom" (2 Sam 15:13).

REFLECTION

David's betrayal by his son Absalom is apparent in a heartrending psalm:

> If an enemy had reviled me,
> > I could have borne it;
> If he who hates me had vaunted himself against me,
> > I might have hidden from him.
> But you, my other self,
> > my companion and my bosom friend!
> You, whose comradeship I enjoyed;
> > at whose side I walked in procession in the house of God!
>
> (Ps 55:13-15)

Such is the hurt Jesus suffers when members of his body—his "other self"—betray him by divisions among themselves. "We should put an end to . . . division immediately. Let us fall down before our master and implore his mercy with our tears. Then he will be reconciled to us and restore us to the practice of [familial] love that befits us" (St. Clement of Rome, pope).[98]

The sacrament of reconciliation opens the "gates of justice" (Ps 118:19), through which our likeness to God's image is embraced by Christ as his "other self."

QUESTION FOR YOUR REFLECTION

God is the communion of three divine persons in whose image we have been created. Why is refusal to acknowledge one's sinfulness a betrayal of that communion?

TUESDAY

WORD

> *"My son, Absalom! My son, my son, Absalom!"* (2 Sam 19:1).

REFLECTION

Absalom's betrayal fails to silence his father's love for him. Knowing that earthly reconciliation is no longer possible, David sobs tears of wrenching pain at the news of his son's death.

David's tears speak of a "terrible beauty." They tell of a communion that bonds hearts in familial love. When betrayal ruptures that bond, tears of grief spring from the depths of God's Trinitarian communion, whose boundless love spills into hearts created for its "terrible beauty."

The oneness of Christ and the members of his body echo God's communion of persons. The love that this communion generates longs to embrace all men and women. "We entreat you, brothers [and sisters]," writes St. Augustine, "as earnestly as we are able, to have charity, not only for one another, but also for those who are outside the Church. . . . Those who are outside the Church are our brothers [and sisters]" (St. Augustine, bishop).[99]

QUESTION FOR YOUR REFLECTION

What is the communion that Holy Communion celebrates?

WEDNESDAY

WORD

"David regretted having numbered the people, and said to the LORD, 'I have sinned grievously'" (2 Sam 24:10).

REFLECTION

When rulers calculate power by the number of their subjects, they miscalculate the meaning of their rule. It is because of this miscalculation that David cries out, "I have sinned grievously."

David is repentant when he remembers that servanthood is the reason for his kingship. And so it remains. God's favor is determined not by the Church's number of communicants but by the servanthood that its communion signifies. God calls rulers not to number peoples but to serve them. Servanthood is the glory and power of rulers.

An ancient document links Christ's glory and power to the Eucharist: "Say over the cup: We give you thanks, Father, for the holy vine of David, your servant, which you have made known to us through Jesus your servant. . . . For glory and the power are yours forever" (*The Teaching of the Twelve Apostles*).[100]

QUESTION FOR YOUR REFLECTION

God is called "Almighty." How is that name betrayed when Christians reckon power by numbers?

THURSDAY

WORD

"Blessed . . . is the [one] at whose door Christ stands and knocks. Our door is faith; if it is strong enough, the whole house is safe" (St. Ambrose, bishop).[101]

REFLECTION

Only one temple will never be destroyed. It is the "house" of God, whose priceless appointments are God's people in the likeness of God. They are priceless because they are the body of Jesus Christ, in whom dwells the fullness of God.

"Here I stand," Jesus pleads, "knocking at the door. If anyone hears me calling and opens the door, I will enter his house and have supper with him, and he with me" (Rev 3:20). The door of each person's life is faith, and "if it is strong enough, the whole house is safe." Why? Because faith is our warmest welcome for God's Son, who longs to make homes of our houses. St. Ambrose exhorts: "Let your door stand open to receive him, unlock your soul to him, offer him a welcome in your mind, and then you will see the riches of simplicity, the treasures of peace and the joy of grace. Throw open the gate of your heart, stand before the sun of everlasting light 'that shines on [all].' "[102]

QUESTION FOR YOUR REFLECTION

St. Ambrose suggests that Christ knocks at our doors when people in need ask for help. What do these people require of our door of faith?

WORD

"Beloved, see what a marvelous thing love is; its perfection is beyond expression" (St. Clement, pope).[103]

REFLECTION

While the perfection of love is "beyond expression" of our lips, it is not beyond the expression of our deeds. When unity is the climax of deeds, we see "what a marvelous thing love is."

Jesus dies on the cross to fulfill his lifelong passion to end conflict and division. On the eve of his violent death he cries out to his Father, "I pray . . . that all may be one as you, Father, are in me, and I in you; I pray that they may be [one] in us, that the world may believe that you sent me" (John 17:20-21).

Unity, a mark of the Church, is expressed in the wedding of words and deeds. When the world witnesses the integrity of this marriage, all will exclaim, "See what a marvelous thing love is."

QUESTION FOR YOUR REFLECTION

When is unity, a mark of the Church, not "beyond expression"?

WORD

"Jesus . . . is the true peacemaker. . . . [He] made one Church [of Jews and Gentiles] with himself as the cornerstone and, therefore, the true peacemaker" (St. Augustine, bishop).[104]

REFLECTION

Jesus blessed peacemakers rather than peacekeepers (see Matt 5:9). Peacemakers journey with Christ to face harm's makers. They seek not to make war but to make straight the way for reconciliation, whose unity is the perfection of love. This is the "way" of Jesus Christ, Prince of Peace.

Jesus came as peacemaker so that he might be the way of our communion with God and one another. With Christ, peacemakers work for the peace that is yet to be rather than be content with the peace that already is. They offer harm's makers outstretched arms rather than clenched fists. It is in the embrace of peacemakers that Christ reconciles what dissension tears apart.

Peacemakers are evidence of Christ's promise: "Destroy this temple . . . and in three days I will raise it up" (John 2:19).

QUESTION FOR YOUR REFLECTION

Why does peacemaking rather than peacekeeping guarantee future peace?

Fifteenth Week in Ordinary Time

SUNDAY

WORD

"The jar of flour did not go empty, nor the jug of oil run dry, as the LORD had foretold through Elijah" (1 Kgs 17:16).

REFLECTION

Standing above a well and in childlike wonder I asked my uncle, "How far down is this well?"

"Don't ask, how far down," he laughed, "but how far up."

Pointing to his overflowing pail of water, he gazed at the sky and added: "Because this came from up there I'm able to pump it from down there."

And so with Elijah. God's holiness nourishes Elijah's spirit to provide the widow with a year's supply of flour and oil. Given from above, the power of Elijah's holiness lingers below long after he leaves the widow's home.

Today the Church's sacramental wellsprings of holiness call us to the holiness they celebrate. The sacraments nourish when, wrapped in wonder, we approach their never-to-be-spent wells of mystery expecting to be quenched of our never-to-be-spent thirsts for God's holiness.

QUESTION FOR YOUR REFLECTION

Sacraments are mysteries in whom holiness is hidden. What is required if holiness is to become visible?

MONDAY

WORD

"Elijah appealed to all the people and said, 'How long will you straddle the issue?'" (1 Kgs 18:21).

REFLECTION

Quite prophetically someone comments that Christianity comforts the afflicted and afflicts the comfortable.

Elijah sees the smugness of Israel's king and subjects, whose consciences find comfort in worshiping both God and Baal. He afflicts their comfort when he says, "How long will you straddle the issues?"

Genuine prophets disturb all who find comfort mixing truth and error in melting pots that produce only ambiguous identity. The Church's prophetic role brings comfort to the afflicted when it comes to light that the comfortable have been straddling issues. When the Church holds to the truth of each issue, it becomes clear why fence-straddlers are disturbed.

QUESTION FOR YOUR REFLECTION

What issues are straddled in pro-abortion's slogan, freedom of choice?

WORD

"Water, you see, is of no avail for future salvation without the proclamation of the Lord's cross" (St. Ambrose, bishop).[105]

REFLECTION

Writing to Learn is both title and theme of an interesting book.[106] The author contends that those who choose the glory of academic excellence must first bear the cross of "writing to learn."

And so it is for all who seek baptism's promise of holiness. Such excellence radiates from those in whom the cross of Christ has been inscribed. St. Paul asks, "Are you not aware that we who were baptized into Christ Jesus were baptized into his death?" (Rom 6:3).

Jesus comes to us as God's *Word*. He writes that Word by way of his death and resurrection inscribed in each of us. His Word is written in the hearts of all who write their lives by his way of the cross and in that script experience the excellence of his resurrection.

QUESTION FOR YOUR REFLECTION

Water is required for the validity of baptism. What is required for its effectiveness?

WORD

"You were told before not to believe only what you saw" (St. Ambrose, bishop).[107]

REFLECTION

Sacraments are not magic. They signify patterns of Christ's life revealed in Christians who live their significance. Those who complain

"I get nothing out of sacraments" display their need for magic. The nothing they get is the magic sacraments can't give.

"Does this water . . . really have the power to sanctify me?" St. Ambrose asks. He replies, "Learn from this that water does not sanctify without the Holy Spirit."[108] The faith that signifies the Holy Spirit's refreshing and cleansing presence from baptism's waters also signifies the baptismal commitment to live patterns of life consistent with sacramental signs.

"All is new" (2 Cor 5:17) in Christ when sacramental significance has been translated into human significance. Christians become sacraments when they look beyond what sacraments say to their eyes and gaze at what they speak to their hearts.

QUESTION FOR YOUR REFLECTION

What missing link causes the assertion, "I get nothing out of sacraments"?

THURSDAY

WORD

"Seek the word of the LORD at once" (1 Kgs 22:5).

REFLECTION

"God's word is living and effective, sharper than any two-edged sword" (Heb 4:12). This "sword" both cuts and heals when its prophetic presence is clearly seen as the Church's identity. Christ sent the Holy Spirit to anoint the Church with the responsibility of speaking God. For that role the Church must be ready to stand alone whenever its thrust of the "two-edged sword" cuts into this world's disease of injustice.

Wisdom compels the Church to be faithful to its name, "Catholic," a name that means wholeness. The Church is prophetic when its zeal for truth's wholeness gathers diversity into the harmony of universality. When all the colors of diversity harmonize, "Christ sees his Church clothed in white. . . . He cries out, 'How beautiful you are, my beloved, how beautiful you are.' "[109]

QUESTION FOR YOUR REFLECTION

When the Church faces resistance on the issues of life and death, how is this a healthy sign that it is exercising its prophetic role?

WORD

"Trust in the LORD, your God, and you will be found firm. Trust in his prophets and you will succeed" (2 Chr 20:20).

REFLECTION

An associate professor of religion at Columbia University has written: "Religions in America are constantly adapting to popular tastes. . . . Those traditions that resist the prevailing currents of popular opinion—Roman Catholicism's refusal to sanction artificial means of birth control, for instance—face disaffection, even attrition."[110]

Those who are fully aware of the Church's prophetic role are undaunted by prospects of "disaffection" and "attrition" from those who take the well-traveled road of "popular tastes." Rather, they are consoled by twenty centuries of Catholic presence. This stability asserts that "disaffection" and "attrition" are as short-lived as "popular tastes."

The Catholic Church does not rest on a foundation of free-market religion. Its foundation is Jesus Christ, "a stone which the builders rejected that became a cornerstone" (1 Pet 2:7).

QUESTION FOR YOUR REFLECTION

What issues are causing "disaffection" and "attrition" in members and nonmembers of the Catholic Church today?

WORD

> *"Elijah said to Elisha, 'Ask for whatever I may do for you, before I am taken from you.' Elisha answered, 'May I receive a double portion of your spirit' "* (2 Kgs 2:9).

REFLECTION

Authentic prophets care that their words and deeds speak God. They are prophets because they look so intently at the present that they also see the future. They see people whose blindness to God's goodness sends them stumbling into the future.

The Church agonizes. Clothed with the "double portion" of Christ's human and divine identity, the Church agonizes over those who seek "a double portion" of this world's spirit. This is why "the Church . . . exhorts her children, her neighbors to hasten to [her] mysteries: 'Neighbors,' she says, 'come and eat,' . . . 'taste and see that the Lord is good' " (St. Ambrose bishop).[111]

The Eucharist celebrates the "double portion" of Christ's Spirit. "During the meal Jesus took bread, blessed it, broke it, and gave it to his disciples. 'Take this and eat it,' he said, 'this is my body.' Then he took a cup, gave thanks, and gave it to them. 'All of you must drink from it,' he said, 'for this is my blood, the blood of the covenant, to be poured out in behalf of many for the forgiveness of sins' " (Matt 26:26-28).

QUESTION FOR YOUR REFLECTION

Prophets who "fix" their "eyes on Jesus" (Heb 3:1) see the future. Why?

Sixteenth Week in Ordinary Time

WORD

> *"The Father of our Lord Jesus Christ . . . comforts us in all our afflictions and thus enables us to comfort those who are in trouble, with the same consolation we have received from him"* (2 Cor 1:3-4).

REFLECTION

A search for consolation by way of comfort ends in misery for all who are blind to comfort's presence "in all our afflictions." On the eve of his crucifixion Jesus found comfort as he prayed: "My soul is troubled now, yet what should I say—Father, save me from this hour? But it was for this that I came to this hour" (John 12:27).

Jesus saves us not *from* our afflictions but *in* our afflictions. Daily sufferings fill up in our own flesh what is left unfulfilled in his flesh (see Col 1:24). In our sufferings the Father unfolds within us a strength destined to be our comfort. "When cares abound within me," the psalmist rejoices, "your comfort gladdens my soul" (Ps 94:19).

QUESTION FOR YOUR REFLECTION

St. Paul writes, "When I am powerless, it is then that I am strong" (2 Cor 12:10). How does faith resolve this apparent contradiction?

WORD

> *"I urge you to strive to do all things in the harmony of God . . . as a sign and a pattern of eternal life"* (St. Ignatius of Antioch, bishop and martyr).[112]

REFLECTION

Blueprints yield yawns for those who don't "see the picture."

The picture of Jesus Christ is the Church vividly portrayed in the lives of all who picture themselves as the body of Christ. They "do all things in the harmony of God . . . as a sign and a pattern of eternal life."

The "pattern of eternal life" is a life of communion among those who bear the name "Christian." They are the picture of God's communion of persons when their daily lives portray forgiveness, reconciliation, healing, and peacemaking. These are the blueprints of Jesus' way, truth, and life. The communion of believers who are the picture of these blueprints mirrors the picture of eternal life.

QUESTION FOR YOUR REFLECTION

Catechisms offer the blueprints of "one, holy, catholic, and apostolic" as the marks of the Church. What is the picture of these blueprints?

TUESDAY

WORD

"You are my letter, known and read by all . . ., written on your hearts . . . not with ink but by the Spirit of the living God, not on tablets of stone but on tablets of flesh in the heart" (2 Cor 3:2-3).

REFLECTION

Gossip about a pastor's horrendous homilies was silenced when a parishioner replied, "You may be right, but that man's whole life is the best homily I have ever experienced."

Similarly, St. Paul tells the people of Corinth that they are his letter "written on [their] hearts." He sees their lives filled with the "Spirit of the living God," whose presence neither "ink" nor "tablets of stone" can convey.

Pope Paul VI suggests that "modern man listens more willingly to witnesses than to teachers, and if he does listen to teachers it is because they are witnesses."[113] The Word of God is destined to be "written on [our] hearts," because it is from there that Christ longs to be "read" in the pages of his disciples' lives.

This is the "letter" that modern men and women willingly read.

QUESTION FOR YOUR REFLECTION

From either past or present experience, whose life has been the best homily you have ever experienced?

WEDNESDAY

WORD

"Turn to the Lord with your whole heart and leave behind this wretched world. . . . Make room for Christ" (The Imitation of Christ).[114]

REFLECTION

From hearts with room only for earthly treasures comes the wretchedness that mars the world's beauty. The author of *The Imitation of Christ* writes: "God's glory and beauty are within you, and he delights in dwelling there. . . . So come, faithful soul. Prepare your heart for your spouse to dwell within you. . . . Make room for Christ."[115]

Those who "make room for Christ" remove the inner wretchedness that imposes futility on the world. When they "turn to the Lord" they empty their hearts, enabling "the whole created world" to see "the revelation of the sons of God . . . because the world itself will be freed from . . . corruption and share in the glorious freedom of the children of God" (Rom 8:19-21).

"Blest are the single-hearted for they shall see God" (Matt 5:8). When the single-hearted "make room for Christ," they make room for all of creation to give praise and glory to God.

QUESTION FOR YOUR REFLECTION

What futility did Adam and Eve impose on God's creation?

WORD

"We do not fix our gaze on what is seen but on what is unseen. What is seen is transitory; what is unseen lasts forever" (2 Cor 4:18).

REFLECTION

In primitive times the weight of "seen" possessions determined the glory of their possessors. Elevating "glory" and "weight" to a meaning other than bulk, St. Paul offers encouragement to all who are weighed down by the burdens of each day: "Do not lose heart," he exhorts, "because our inner being is renewed each day. . . . The present burden of our trial is light enough, and earns for us an eternal weight of glory beyond all comparison" (2 Cor 4:16-17).

What we possess cannot be compared to the weight of God's peace, joy, and light. These are the treasures of the poor in spirit, whose poverty leaves ample room for the glory of God's presence. Each person's glory is the poverty that welcomes the "unseen" presence of God's kingdom. "How blest are the poor in spirit: the reign of God is theirs" (Matt 5:3).

Praying with the psalmist, St. Ambrose asks, "Why do you turn away your face?" (Ps 44:25). He replies: "We may say it in another way. Even if, Lord, you turn your face away from us, yet 'we are sealed with the glory of your face.' Your glory is in our hearts and shines in the deep places of our spirit. Indeed, no one can live if you turn away your face" (St. Ambrose, bishop).[116]

QUESTION FOR YOUR REFLECTION

Why does "poor in spirit" carry weight with Jesus Christ?

WORD

"For our sakes God made him who did not know sin, to be sin, so that in him we might become the very holiness of God" (2 Cor 5:21).

REFLECTION

Agere sequitur esse. I first met these three Latin words in college and they have been my friends ever since. They translate, "to act follows to be" or, loosely, "what you do flows from who you are."

I find this ageless axiom to be thematic of Pope John Paul II's encyclical commemorating Pope Leo XIII's 1892 landmark letter on labor. He writes: "God has imprinted his own image and likeness on man (cf. Gen 1:26), conferring upon him an incomparable dignity. . . . In effect, beyond the rights which man acquires by his own work, there exist rights which do not correspond to any work . . . but which flow from his essential dignity as a person."[117]

The "essential dignity" of each person! This is "the very holiness of God." From this dignity follows the essential action of each human being graced to be "the very holiness of God." "If anyone is in Christ," writes St. Paul, "he is a new creation. . . . All this has been done by God, who has reconciled us to himself through Christ and has given us the ministry of reconciliation" (2 Cor 5:17-18). The holiness of our being leads us to deeds of reconciliation.

QUESTION FOR YOUR REFLECTION

If the opposite axiom, Who you are flows from what you do, is true, how is the meaning of freedom changed?

WORD

"As your fellow workers we beg you not to receive the grace of God in vain" (2 Cor 6:1).

REFLECTION

Hearts shrivel when their desire is praise for tasks done. Hearts are enlarged when their only desire is to proclaim the greatness of the Lord (see Luke 1:46).

God has graced us not to proclaim the greatness of our tasks but to become ministers of God's love. "God is love, and he who abides in love abides in God, and God in him" (1 John 4:16).

Love *is* God's identity. God created all of us to *be* that identity and *do* works of love to "proclaim the greatness of the Lord."

Time spent seeking only praise for accomplishments is senseless, purposeless, vain. To accept God's grace to be ministers of God's love is to live in a time acceptable to God.

QUESTION FOR YOUR REFLECTION

Who "receives the grace of God in vain"?

Seventeenth Week in Ordinary Time

SUNDAY

WORD

"Make room for us in your hearts" (2 Cor 7:2).

REFLECTION

St. Paul's plea, "make room for us in your hearts," reflects his grasp of communion's meaning. He asks the Corinthians to "make room in [their] hearts" not for himself alone but *for us*. He asks room for God and for all the saints whose communion he shares.

St. Paul wants the love of others because his heart has been enlarged by Christ's longing for the communion that makes humankind one in Christ. This wholeness is the holiness celebrated in the Eucharist's Holy Communion. It signifies a love that enlarges our hearts to make room for the presence of God's communion with *everyone!*

Holy Communion is the sacrament of God's "plan he was pleased to decree in Christ, to be carried out in the fullness of time: namely, to bring all things in the heavens and on earth into one under Christ's headship" (Eph 1:9-10).

QUESTION FOR YOUR REFLECTION

In the light of Holy Communion's fullest sacramental meaning, what commitment is required for the "Amen" response to "Body of Christ"?

MONDAY

WORD

"Yes, there is mercy in heaven, but the road to it is paved by our merciful acts on earth" (St. Caesarius of Arles, bishop).[118]

REFLECTION

A photographer awaited the mercy of friendly rescue from his sand-locked car in Saudi Arabia. At the approach of an Iraqi tank, however, he visualized himself as a victim of revenge.

Amazement replaced terror as the Iraqi pulled the young man's car from the desert sand and, with upraised arms, asked the photographer only for mercy.

This moment of wedding between these two mercies touched the lives of millions of TV viewers. In the desert wilderness Christ's plea is for the willing exchange of two mercies shriven of all revenge, for "blest are they who show mercy; mercy shall be theirs" (Matt 5:7). Whenever these words are heard, heaven and earth meet.

Merciful acts pave the way to heaven's throne of mercy. God exchanges forgiveness for our humble confession, "O God, be merciful to me, a sinner" (Luke 18:13).

QUESTION FOR YOUR REFLECTION

How do we "prepare the way of the Lord" (Isa 40:3)?

TUESDAY

WORD

"He who supplies seed for the sower and bread for the eater will provide in abundance; he will multiply the seed you sow and increase your generous yield" (2 Cor 9:10).

REFLECTION

The Dead Sea surrenders its bounty only to the sun's burning rays. It hoards within its boundaries all it receives from the Jordan River. That sea's selfishness is why it's named "Dead."

Selfishness is deadly because it forgets the source of bounty. Such lapse of memory reaps the bounty of loneliness inhabiting the poverty of pride. "Poor . . . you certainly are," writes St. Basil the Great, "[because] you are poor in love, generosity, faith in God and hope of eternal happiness."[119]

Jesus spent much time at the Sea of Galilee, where every drop of the Jordan's bounty is dispensed for the needs of all. It is of this kind of generosity that Jesus speaks: "Give, and it shall be given to you. Good measure pressed down, shaken together, running over, will they pour into the fold of your garment. For the measure you measure with will be measured back to you" (Luke 6:38).

QUESTION FOR YOUR REFLECTION

The right to private property does not confer the right to *absolute* ownership. Why?

WEDNESDAY

WORD

"We do indeed live in the body but we do not wage war with human resources" (2 Cor 10:3).

REFLECTION

Mary gave her word to God: "I am the servant of the Lord. Let it be done to me as you say" (Luke 1:38). In response to Mary's obedience, "The Word became flesh and made his dwelling among us" (John 1:14).

Obedience does not demand degradation. It opens the door of faith, enabling us to become instruments of God's Word seeking to reveal God's kingdom in our humanity. The Holy Spirit looks for our consent to speak Mary's word, "I am the servant of the Lord. Let it be done to me as you say."

The Word of God obediently becomes Eucharistic presence. This obedience likewise obligates our presence for worship. In the union of heaven and earth the Word is enfleshed in bread and wine and in all who gather so that the Word of God might be kept.

QUESTION FOR YOUR REFLECTION

Why is our presence at the Eucharist obligatory?

THURSDAY

WORD

"While the rulers of the different nations have limits to their sovereignty, the holy Catholic Church alone has a power without boundaries throughout the entire world. For, as Scripture says: God 'has made peace her border' " (St. Cyril of Jerusalem, bishop).[120]

REFLECTION

The Catholic Church has no boundaries except the peace that knows no boundaries. It prays, "Lord, may this sacrifice, which has made our peace with you, advance the peace and salvation of all the world."[121]

In this prayer the Church charts sacrifice as the way we enable Christ to "advance the peace and salvation of all the world." Why is sacrifice the way of peace?

The Prince of Peace faces hostility because he reaches out to embrace the poor. Obediently awaiting crucifixion, he says to all of his disciples: "My peace is my gift to you; I do not give it to you as the world gives peace" (John 14:27).

How does Christ give his peace? "I assure you, as often as you did it for one of my least brothers, you did it for me" (Matt 25:40).

QUESTION FOR YOUR REFLECTION

"I depend on the Eucharist," some say. In what way does the Eucharist depend upon us "to advance the peace and salvation of all the world"?

FRIDAY

WORD

"I am content with weakness, with mistreatment, with distress, with persecutions and difficulties for the sake of Christ; for when I am powerless, it is then that I am strong" (2 Cor 12:10).

REFLECTION

For St. Paul, God's glory is the "treasure we possess in earthen vessels, to make it clear that its surpassing power comes from God and not from us" (2 Cor 4:7). His faith links him to Christ's anguished cry, "My God, my God, why have you forsaken me?" (Mark 15:34). His faith is strengthened when he remembers that Christ was raised from the dead.

Christ's cry of abandonment echoes down the centuries in the cries of the powerless. St. Paul longs for the powerless to understand, in the light of Christ's death and resurrection, that their weaknesses and God's strength are devotion's solid rock.

St. Polycarp was praised for such devotion: "Recognizing your devotion to God, firmly built as if on a solid rock, I am full of thanksgiving for allowing me to see [you]." He was encouraged to "carry the burdens of all . . . as the Lord carries yours. . . . The greater the toil the greater the reward" (St. Ignatius of Antioch, bishop and martyr).[122]

101

QUESTION FOR YOUR REFLECTION

St. Paul has written, "I will do no boasting about myself unless it be about my weaknesses" (2 Cor 12:5). Why is weakness the source of hope?

SATURDAY

WORD

"Work together in harmony, struggle together, run together, suffer together, rest together, as stewards, advisors and servants of God" (St. Ignatius of Antioch, bishop and martyr).[123]

REFLECTION

In *The Search for an American Public Theology* the author laments the abandonment of common understandings concerning ethical standards of public policy. He writes: "If there is no body of shared meanings in a society, there is no sense of moral obligation, either. In such a situation, tolerance, justice, charity, and all the other civic virtues which are essential to the functioning of a truly pluralistic society will wither away, leaving only self-interest as the determinant of public policy. And there is little which is more intolerant than pure self-interest."[124]

St. Paul ends his Second Letter to the Corinthians cautioning those who oblige themselves to self-interest. "I fear I may find discord, jealousy, outbusts of anger, selfish ambitions, slander and gossip, self-importance, disorder" (2 Cor 12:20).

If there is harmony among us, we have proof that our society is bonded by common understandings that transcend the narrow boundaries of self-interest. Christ provides these common understandings.

QUESTION FOR YOUR REFLECTION

What is the fate of freedom when public policy is based solely on self-interest's appeal to private choice?

Trinity Sunday

WORD

"The Spirit we have received is not the world's spirit but God's spirit, helping us to recognize the gifts he has given us" (1 Cor 2:12).

REFLECTION

Referring to Pentecost Sunday, a student asks, "Why does the Church assign only one day to the Holy Spirit?"

Quite to the contrary, every day of Ordinary Time is assigned to the Holy Spirit, guiding us to recognize the companionship of God's trinity of persons. The first Pentecost entitles each day to be time's home for the timeless companionship of God's trinity of persons.

For that reason the Church does not neglect any person of God's identity, especially God's Spirit, who daily "help[s] us to recognize the gifts [God] has given." Creativeness is God-Creator's gift. Salvation is God-Savior's gift. Wholeness is God-Spirit's gift. This trinity of gifts is ours because we are the likeness of God's trinity of persons.

We are baptized to be sacraments of God's gifts. We are sacraments of God-Creator when the gift of creativeness compels us to invite from others the beauty, truth, and goodness hidden in their mystery. We are sacraments of God-Savior when our lives interpret the meaning of Christ's saving passover from "the world's spirit" to a wisdom "eye has not seen, ear has not heard" (1 Cor 2:9). We are sacraments of God-Spirit when the gift of wholeness urges us to be agents of the reconciliation whose wholeness bears the fruit of holiness.

QUESTION FOR YOUR REFLECTION

The Church acknowledges God's trinity of persons each day. Why is every day a "Pentecost"?

The Body and Blood of Christ
(Corpus Christi)

SUNDAY AFTER TRINITY SUNDAY

WORD

"When Moses came to the people and related all the words and ordinances of the LORD, they all answered with one voice, 'We will do everything that the LORD has told us'" (Exod 24:3).

REFLECTION

Centuries of silence elapse before God replies to Israel's resolve to "do everything that the LORD has told us." Jesus breaks the silence. At the Last Supper, after he breaks bread and gives it to his disciples, he charges them to "do this as a remembrance of me" (Luke 22:19). His reply breaks through walls of "words and ordinances" and reveals God's longing for intimacy: "This is my body to be given for you. Do this as a remembrance of me."

This "remembrance" means more than recollections of a past event. The sacrament of Corpus Christi—Body of Christ—is a re-membering of those who have been baptized *to be* the body of Christ. This event in sacrament is the event Jesus invites us to become in reality. The body that we eat as bread is the body that we *are* as members of Christ's body, the Church.

God's longing for intimacy can be felt in Isaiah's prophetic utterance: "The Lord himself will give you this sign: the virgin shall be with child, and bear a son, and shall name him Immanuel" (Isa 7:14). Immanuel—God with us—and the son's birth from a virgin's flesh and blood reverberates throughout the centuries, crying out God's longing for us to be the flesh and blood of Christ's presence re-membered in word and sacrament. "Do this as a remembrance of me" are words of sacrament becoming to us, for we are the reality of Corpus Christi.

104

QUESTION FOR YOUR REFLECTION

Jesus asks Peter, "Who do you say that I am?" (Matt 16:15). But who does Jesus say that *we* are?

Sacred Heart

FRIDAY AFTER THE SECOND SUNDAY
AFTER PENTECOST

WORD

"I am certain that neither death nor life, neither angels nor principalities, neither the present nor the future, nor powers, neither height nor depth nor any other creature, will be able to separate us from the love of God that comes to us in Christ Jesus, our Lord" (Rom 8:38-39).

REFLECTION

At one time Catholic homes featured the picture of a fiery heart and the caption Sacred Heart of Jesus. While the devotional intent of such displays is understandable, its subtle suggestion of love apart from its human dwelling place is not. Sensing this suggestion's debasement of Christ's incarnation, the Church counter-suggested that the Sacred Heart be pictured with Christ's body to affirm his solidarity with all men and women and their destiny to form Corpus Christi, the body of Christ.

One's heart is not merely another member of the body. Upon the heart rests the vitality and the survival of all bodily members. When heartbeats cease, the earthly life of each person ceases. How grotesque to picture hearts apart from their reason to exist!

"God is love, and he who abides in love abides in God, and God in him" (1 John 4:16). As Son of God, Jesus is with us as God's identity. Love is not a function God does; love is the identity God is. Love is at the heart of God's essence, the essence that, in Christ, spills out into all humanity and gets to the heart of who we are and why we exist.

Jesus is the heart that bonds all men and women to God and to one another. This communion is as necessary for life's vitality and survival as the communion of heart with the bodily members it keeps alive. This is why St. Paul writes: "I am certain that . . . [no] other creature will be able to separate us from the love of God that comes to us in Christ Jesus, our Lord."

QUESTION FOR YOUR REFLECTION

Why is the feast of Christ's Sacred Heart celebrated shortly after the feast of Corpus Christi?

Eighteenth Week in Ordinary Time

SUNDAY

WORD

"Greetings, sons and daughters. . . . I am now convinced and fully aware that I have learned much by speaking with you . . . and so I am driven in all ways to love you more than my own life" (attributed to Barnabas).[125]

REFLECTION

Jesus points the way to self-esteem: "You shall love your neighbor as yourself" (Mark 12:31).

Is it rash to imply that self-love measures our love for God and neighbor? Not if faith compels us to see and love in ourselves what God sees and loves in us. What does God see in us? Our likeness to God's image. As we are drawn to this beauty in ourselves, we lovingly open ourselves to God and neighbor. "In the measure you give you shall receive, and more besides" (Mark 4:24).

To love one's self is to cherish the esteem God has for us. This is the esteem that compels Barnabas to assert, "I am driven in all ways to love you more than my own life." He sees limitless treasuries of self-worth to be found in his loving service to others.

QUESTION FOR YOUR REFLECTION

What is the difference between self-love and self-indulgence?

WORD

> *"God has abolished the sacrifice of the old law so that the new law of our Lord Jesus Christ, which does not bind by slavish compulsion, might have an offering not made by man"* (attributed to Barnabas).[126]

REFLECTION

When Jesus is asked, "Are you 'He who is to come' or do we look for someone else?" (Luke 7:20) he replies, "Go and report to John what you have seen and heard. The blind recover their sight, cripples walk, lepers are cured, the deaf hear, dead men are raised to life, and the poor have the good news preached to them" (Luke 7:22).

Catholic identity is not a problem as long as its prime pursuit is "the new law of our Lord Jesus Christ." That "new law" compels us to care for the needs of the poor. Those needs are universal, and the Church will be catholic as long as it cares for the poor and oppressed all over the world.

St. Mark hints at the Church's identity when he says, "Jesus saw a vast crowd. He pitied them, for they were like sheep without a shepherd" (Mark 6:34). Shepherd! That is the Church's identity.

QUESTION FOR YOUR REFLECTION

Jesus says, "I have come, not to abolish [the law and the prophets], but to fulfill them" (Matt 5:17). What law of Jesus fulfills "the law and the prophets"?

WORD

"To Amos, Amaziah said: 'Off with you, visionary, flee to the land of Judah! There earn your bread by prophesying, but never again prophesy in Bethel; for it is the king's sanctuary and a royal temple" (Amos 7:12-13).

REFLECTION

True prophets are rarely tolerated. They are despised by masters of deceit because they expose the lies about humankind's wholeness being solely from within this world's boundaries. Prophets hold fast to human dignity, which knows no boundaries.

True prophets speak about wholeness with God. This wholeness rests on justice and its unyielding defense of human dignity's *eternal* worth. As long as the Church proclaims the voice of justice, voices of deceit will shriek, "Off with you, visionary!"

The Church insists that Jesus Christ is the identity that *justifies* human worth. He found this justification so valuable that he willingly shed a prophet's blood for all.

QUESTION FOR YOUR REFLECTION

"What is this person worth?" How does the world answer this question? How does God answer it?

WORD

"Share with your neighbor whatever you have, and so not say of anything, this is mine" (attributed to Barnabas).[127]

REFLECTION

When Mother Teresa takes food to the poor, she is struck by their instinctive response: they share it with those they deem poorer than themselves.

God's grace is amazingly witnessed by the God-like generosity of the poor. In their deprivation of life's necessities they feel a solidarity with all of the poor. They live Barnabas' message, "Share with your neighbor whatever you have, and so not say of anything this is mine."

The Church teaches that private property is not an *absolute* right. What is absolute is God's generous gift of imperishable life and his will that we share the abundance of earthly life's perishable gifts. "Such then is the way of light."[128]

QUESTION FOR YOUR REFLECTION

What is the fallacy of the claim that the right to private property is an absolute right?

THURSDAY

WORD

"We lay aside [earthly] likeness and put on [heavenly] likeness. . . . That is why [the LORD] says: 'Set me as a seal upon your heart' " (Baldwin, bishop of Canterbury).[129]

REFLECTION

Ten Auschwitz prisoners were condemned to execution after an escape. Franciscan father Maximilian Maria Kolbe pointed to one of the condemned and said: "I would like to take that man's place. He has a wife and children."[130] The Nazi commandant complied. Father Kolbe, after suffering many days of starvation, died in place of the husband and parent.

The love of this sainted man gives proof of love's victory over death. "Death is strong," writes the bishop of Canterbury, "[but] love too is strong, for it can conquer death itself, soothe its sting, calm its violence, and bring its victory to naught. The time will come when death is reviled and taunted: 'O death, where is your sting? O death, where is your victory?' "[131]

The love that spares life is but a ray of the sun compared to the death of God's Son on the cross. By his death and resurrection, Jesus gives proof in the darkness of death's night that "God is love" (1 John 4:8). In the light of such love St. John pleads, "Let us love in deed and in truth and not merely talk about it" (1 John 3:18).

QUESTION FOR YOUR REFLECTION

What "sting" did Adam and Eve suffer in Eden's garden? What was the "sting" of Christ when he died on the tree of life?

FRIDAY

WORD

"One should not wonder that the soul is capable of so sublime an activity. . . [that] it should share the understanding, knowledge and love which God achieves in himself" (St. John of the Cross, priest).[132]

REFLECTION

Pulled to his feet by Peter and James, a cripple walks for the first time in his life. Those who witness this marvel, "utterly stupefied at what had happened" (Acts 3:10), adore the two apostles.

Embarrassed, Peter asks the crowd, "Why does this surprise you? Why do you stare at us as if we had made this man walk by some power or holiness of our own? . . . God raised him from the dead, and we are his witnesses" (Acts 3:12, 15).

No marvel seen by the eye outweighs the faith to accept the glory of being instruments for God's wonderful works. Lives at the service of Christ mirror his marvels. About this, St. John of the Cross states simply, "The soul united to God and transformed in him draws from within God a divine breath, much like the most high God himself. . . . This is what takes place in those who have achieved perfection."[133]

QUESTION FOR YOUR REFLECTION

Why is focus only on marvelous deeds a sign of misdirected faith?

WORD

"It is love that I desire, not sacrifice, and knowledge of God rather than holocausts" (Hos 6:6).

REFLECTION

A Sunday preface for Ordinary Time declares, "So great was your love that you gave us your Son as our redeemer. You sent him as one like ourselves, though free from sin, that you might see and love in us what you see and love in Christ."[134]

Nothing matches the glory of mirroring the identity of Christ. We have been created for that purpose and God expects us to fulfill it. St. Iranaeus writes, "God demanded . . . not sacrifices and holocausts, but faith, obedience and righteousness. God expressed his will when he taught them in the words of Hosea, 'I desire mercy more than sacrifice, the knowledge of God more than holocausts' " (St. Iranaeus, bishop).[135]

Sacred signs come to life when we live what they celebrate. When we celebrate sacraments conscious that we are the body of Christ, God sees and loves "in us what [God] sees and loves in Christ."

QUESTION FOR YOUR REFLECTION

God does not desire ritual for the sake of ritual. What is ritual's reality that God desires to "see and love in us"?

Nineteenth Week in Ordinary Time

WORD

"It would be no consolation for me to enjoy your life if your holy people stood in death" (St. Catherine of Siena, virgin.[136]

REFLECTION

Thanks to the Polish, the word "solidarity" is used worldwide. In the fourteenth century St. Catherine of Siena, grasps its meaning. This great saint reasons that she is linked to all of humanity because of its communion with God's communion of persons. She sees her sins degrading all; she also sees her acts of love bonding all.

"When you created man," she prays, "you were moved by love to make him in your own image and likeness."[137] For St. Catherine, God's communion of three persons is the rationale for humankind's solidarity.

The solidarity of love between God and ourselves is also the solidarity of love between ourselves and others.

QUESTION FOR YOUR REFLECTION

Why do we confess our sins to a priest?

MONDAY

WORD

"Of his own free will Jesus ran to meet those sufferings that were foretold in the scriptures concerning him. . . . All this he endured in working out our salvation" (Theodoret of Cyr, bishop).[138]

REFLECTION

Americans rejoiced when determined rescuers raced against time to save a small child trapped in a well. Their determination bonded the people of America. In the truest sense what had happened to the child happened to all. Likewise, what had been done for the child had been done for all. Solidarity united us.

The rescue of a small child and its impact on this nation's solidarity is but an echo of Jesus' determination to be the sacrament of his name, "Savior." Jesus' sufferings reflect his Father's passion for us to share a happiness that "eye has not seen, ear has not heard" (1 Cor 2:9).

No one is created to be alone. It was for eternal solidarity against eternal aloneness that Jesus eagerly "stepped forward and presented

112

himself to those who came in search of him, saying: 'I am the one you are looking for.' "[139]

QUESTION FOR YOUR REFLECTION

Solidarity and solitary are poles apart. Why does the passion to possess this world's perishables make us solitaries?

WORD

"When a shepherd sees that his sheep have scattered, he keeps one of them under control and leads it to the pastures he chooses, and thus he draws the other sheep back to him by means of the one" (Theodoret of Cyr, bishop).[140]

REFLECTION

With a magnet, the mother gathered pins and needles that her small son had carelessly scattered across the living-room floor. The boy, with childlike awe, wondered at the magnet's power to gather.

Awe also draws the poor to Jesus, whose sense of justice draws him to them. Jesus longs to gather all whose lives are scattered by the architects of injustice. Love for the poor is the magnetic power that gathers the poor to "the LORD our justice" (Jer 23:6).

In every age the Church begs us to "fix your eyes on Jesus" (Heb 3:1), whose presence can be found wherever there is poverty of body, mind, or spirit. Likewise, when the Church is found among the poor, the eyes of all are drawn to its presence there. The Church is magnetic when what it teaches is what it does.

QUESTION FOR YOUR REFLECTION

What is the magnetism of Mother Teresa of Calcutta?

113

WORD

"He shall judge between many peoples
and impose terms on strong and distant nations;
They shall beat their swords into plowshares,
and their spears into pruning hooks;
One nation shall not raise the sword against another,
nor shall they train for war again" (Mic 4:3).

REFLECTION

Instruments of war are not peacemakers. War begets war, while justice begets justice. Those who perfect instruments of war are also driven to the perfection of war. Those who are driven to the perfection of justice are also driven to the perfection of peace.

In the eyes of God, justice is the peacemaker. The day of peace arrives when nations replace war with peace as the term for the judgment of "strong and distant nations." Peace is at hand when nations cry out:

I will gather the lame,
And I will assemble the outcasts,
and those whom I have afflicted.
I will make of the lame a remnant,
and of those driven far off a strong nation (Mic 4:6-7).

QUESTION FOR YOUR REFLECTION

How is peace made?

WORD

"Since we think of Christ as our peace, we may call ourselves true Christians only if our lives express Christ by our own peace" (St. Gregory of Nyssa, bishop).[141]

REFLECTION

When Vladimir Horowitz ended his rendition of Rachmaninoff's *Second Piano Concerto,* his electrified listeners leaped to their feet and roared ten minutes of approval, evidence that they had caught the resemblance between Rachmaninoff's intent and Horowitz's performance. The moment celebrated authenticity.

St. Gregory of Nyssa claims that the name "Christian" rings authentic when the masterpiece of God's vision for human dignity is revealed in our performance of that vision. God who is peace envisions us to be peacemakers; God who is light envisions us to be its rays; God who is holiness envisions us to be saints.

We deserve the name Christian only when our lives are masterful renditions of Jesus Christ, God's masterpiece of peace, light, and holiness.

QUESTION FOR YOUR REFLECTION

What person in your life deserves the name Christian?

FRIDAY

WORD

> *"With what shall I come before the LORD, and bow before God most high?"* (Mic 6:6).

REFLECTION

Jesus is asked, "Lord, are they few in number who are to be saved?" He replies: "Try to come in through the narrow door. Many, I tell you, will try to enter and be unable" (Luke 13:23-24).

Salvation's door is narrow because it requires only that God "might see and love in us what [God sees and loves] in Christ."[142] Union with Jesus Christ enables us to enter salvation's "narrow door." .

Christ prays that we might be one with him as he is one with his Father (see John 17:21ff.). How wearisome, then, God finds the prayer he denounces:

Shall I come before him with holocausts,
    with calves a year old?
Will the LORD be pleased with thousands of rams,
    with myriad streams of oil?
Shall I give my first-born for my crime,
    the fruit of my body for the sin of my soul?" (Mic 6:6-7).

QUESTION FOR YOUR REFLECTION

You can't take it with you, runs the saying. What can you take with you?

SATURDAY

WORD

"We shall not die anymore. Even if we fall asleep in this body, we shall live in Christ, as he said: 'Whoever believes in me, even if he die, shall live'" (St. Pacian, bishop).[143]

REFLECTION

Christ is emphatic: "I came that they might have life and have it to the full" (John 10:10). Death, then, is passage to the fullest possession of life. Infants are delivered from the wombs of their mothers into this world. Death delivers us from the womb of this world into the fullness of eternal life.

We are baptized for this deliverance. "I solemnly assure you," says Jesus to Nicodemus, "no one can enter into God's kingdom without being begotten of water and Spirit" (John 3:5). As surely as water quenches earthly thirst, so baptism's faith quenches thirst for the possession of endless life.

"Lord, for your faithful people life is changed, not ended. When the body of our earthly dwelling lies in death we gain an everlasting place in heaven."[144]

QUESTION FOR YOUR REFLECTION

By his redemption, Christ reowned us for God. What attitude toward death does baptism require that we disown?

116

Twentieth Week in Ordinary Time

WORD

" 'Holy, holy, holy is the LORD of hosts!' they cried one to the other. 'All the earth is filled with his glory!' " (Isa 6:3).

REFLECTION

The inference that private choice is the source and summit of sanctity erodes the freedom it purports to defend. Choice is wholly free when it wholly embraces the source and summit of human life.

Isaiah hears heaven's Seraphic choir sing, "Holy, holy, holy is the LORD of hosts. . . . All the earth is filled with his glory!" Here is heaven's assertion that holiness comes from a source beyond the boundaries of private choice. It responds to the deepest yearnings of all men and women for the peace and joy of being "filled with [God's] glory."

In its Eucharistic Prayers, the Church praises God as humanity's primary choice: "Lord, you are holy indeed, the fountain of all holiness," and "Father, you are holy indeed, and all creation rightly gives you praise. All life, all holiness comes from you through your Son, Jesus Christ our Lord, by the working of the Holy Spirit."[145]

QUESTION FOR YOUR REFLECTION

What is the inconsistency between "sanctity" of private choice and "All the earth is filled with [God's] glory"?

WORD

"It is the characteristic of holy men [and women] that their own painful trials do not make them lose their concern for the well-being of others" (St. Gregory the Great, pope).[146]

REFLECTION

Florida's late Senator Claude Pepper is not easily forgotten. In his nineties and with his infirmities this stalwart legislator spent himself in behalf of America's growing population of indigent elderly. He died in this pursuit.

If holiness is gauged by one's frequent "performance" of pious acts with the demeanor of "political correctness" that accompanies them, Senator Pepper may not qualify, but if by his sense of solidarity with the indigent, then he died a holy man. Such solidarity is wholly consistent with God's image. Our likeness to that image qualifies us to be instruments of God's justice, with its passion to defend human dignity at every stage of human life. Those who sense this justice "do not . . . lose their concern for the well-being of others" despite "their own painful trials."

QUESTION FOR YOUR REFLECTION

Holiness as wholeness defines sanctity. Why?

TUESDAY

WORD

"Listen, O house of David! Is it not enough for you to weary men, must you also weary my God?" (Isa 7:13).

REFLECTION

God longs for us to let God be God. When the king of Judah is invited to "ask for a sign from the LORD, your God; let it be deep as the nether world, or high as the sky!" (Isa 7:10), he wearies God with the reply "I will not tempt the LORD" (Isa 7:12).

God ignores the king's veto. "The virgin shall be with child, and bear a son, and shall name him Immanuel" (Isa 7:14).

Impossible? Yes, if divine possibilities are measured by human standards. But if God is Immanuel—God is with us—human measurements of possibility weary God. Should God's presence be limited *only* to human reckonings of divine possibility? Cries of impossibility place God on the level of human endeavor, and we weary God by our refusal to believe.

QUESTION FOR YOUR REFLECTION

What is the significance of the Virgin Mary's birth of Jesus for our daily practice of faith?

WEDNESDAY

WORD

"You may think past ages were good, but it is only because you are not living in them" (St. Augustine, bishop).[147]

REFLECTION

"If only we could go back to the way things were!" Such nostalgia bears the fruit of the ancient skill of grumbling. Although nostalgia poses as remembrance, it imposes on remembrance its forgetfulness of the sorrows that give birth to joys worth remembering.

Those who remember sorrow's birth of joy give thanks for the freedom that refuses to forget sorrow's parentage. All who give thanks for sorrow embrace the Savior, who cried out on the cross, "My God, my God, why have you forsaken me?" (Mark 15:34). The Savior we embrace on the cross is the Savior we embrace at the door of his empty tomb.

At the first Eucharist Jesus asks his disciples to embrace his death and resurrection. He gives only one command: "Do this as a remembrance of me" (Luke 22:19).

QUESTION FOR YOUR REFLECTION

What is the difference between nostalgia and remembrance?

WORD

*"There shall be a highway for the remnant of his people
. . . as there was for Israel when he came up from the land
of Egypt"* (Isa 11:16).

REFLECTION

When Jesus speaks of himself as "the way," he is speaking of justice enfleshed in his person as the way to peace.

Jesus is our justice because his "marvelous exchange" of divinity for humanity *justifies* the reason for the dignity that humanity deserves. Jesus makes humanity deserving because God creates it to be the image and likeness of God. For all time Jesus owns our humanity so that humanity might own his way, his truth, and his life.

Jesus' way of living humanity justifies human life above and beyond this world's ways of being happy.

"Not by appearance shall he judge,
nor by hearsay shall he decide,
But he shall judge the poor with justice,
and decide aright for the land's afflicted (Isa 11:3-4).

QUESTION FOR YOUR REFLECTION

How can Christ's words "How blest are the poor in spirit" (Matt 5:3) be justified?

WORD

*"For the LORD is a God of justice:
blessed are all who wait for him!"* (Isa 30:18).

REFLECTION

Affluence paves the way to impatience because this world's possessions cannot still hearts longing for peace.

Why must we wait for God? Because God is waiting for us to be "poor in spirit" with this beatitude's wisdom of acknowledging that "only in God is my soul at rest" (Ps 62:2). We wait for God because God is waiting for us to "taste and see how good the LORD is" (Ps 34:9).

God waits for us to "taste and see" God's hidden depths in our humanity. This is the peace of heaven with joys that affluence cannot provide. God's favor comes as the Prince of Peace, whose communion with humanity opens the way for communion with his divinity. "The LORD is waiting to show you favor, and he rises to pity you; for the LORD is a God of justice: blessed are all who wait for him!" (Isa 30:18).

QUESTION FOR YOUR REFLECTION

"The LORD is waiting to show you favor." What is this "favor"?

SATURDAY

WORD

"Christ is the atonement for all, the redemption for all"
(St. Ambrose, bishop).[148]

REFLECTION

It is comic to imagine paying for a farm one has inherited. It is tragic when people pay for a redemption already atoned for and bequeathed through Jesus Christ.

The sacrament of baptism does not require us to atone for the sinfulness we have inherited. "Christ is the atonement for all." Baptism requires us to live human life in the way Jesus Christ lived it. We are authentic Christians when we accept the responsibility of living Christ's way of revealing truth and life.

Jesus speaks about the responsibility of living his way: "As the Father has loved me, so I have loved you. Live on in my love" (John 15:9). Living Christ's way of loving is the price of redemption's inheritance.

121

Twenty-first Week in Ordinary Time

SUNDAY

WORD

"On this earth the kingdom is already present in sign;
when the Lord comes it will reach its completion."[149]

REFLECTION

" 'Lord, when my brother wrongs me, how often must I forgive him? Seven times?' 'No,' Jesus replied, 'not seven times; I say, seventy times seven times' " (Matt 18:21-22).

In this exchange one of Peter's absolutes collapses before the generosity of Christ's compassion. For Peter, the generosity of forgiveness ends at the boundary line of "seven times." In the mind of Jesus Christ, then as now, forgiveness flows from a love not measured by numbers.

Is seven the sacramental limitation of sacredness? Quite the opposite. The significance of seven sacraments declares that everything is sacred. The seven sacraments want us to open the eyes of faith to the presence of God in all of creation. With this discovery we see all of creation as the new creation awaiting "its completion."

QUESTION FOR YOUR REFLECTION

How is the environment's pollution evidence that the loss of a sense of sacredness abounds?

122

WORD

*"I will leave as a remnant in your midst a people humble
and lowly, who shall take refuge in the name of the LORD;
the remnant of Israel"* (Zeph 3:12, 13).

REFLECTION

Mary was called to be the mother of Jesus because she was lowly.
She exclaims, "For he has looked upon his servant in her lowliness"
(Luke 1:48).

She confirms the pertinence of the question, Whom does God favor?
She points to humility as the womb for Christ's earthly presence. Mary
senses that the poor in spirit are linked to Christ, who "was known to
be of human estate, . . . humbled himself, obediently accepting even
death, death on a cross!" (Phil 2:7-8).

The humble enjoy God's favor because "the love of God has been
poured out in our hearts through the Holy Spirit" (Rom 5:5). God's love
links us to Jesus, to whom his Father said, "You are my beloved Son.
On you my favor rests" (Luke 3:22). As the love of God was "poured
out" into the lowly virgin's womb, so shall Jesus Christ fill the lowly
with his presence.

QUESTION FOR YOUR REFLECTION

Why is humility linked to God's "favor"?

WORD

*"The paths of repentance . . . are numerous and quite
varied and all lead to heaven"* (St. John Chrysostom,
bishop).[150]

REFLECTION

St. John Chrysostom names five paths to repentance. He begins with the "condemnation of [our] own sins."[151] This step echoes Jesus' plea, "Remove the plank from your own eye first; then you will see clearly to take the speck from your brother's eye" (Matt 7:5).

Forgiveness is a second path: "Put out of your minds the harm done us by our enemies in order to master our anger, and to forgive our fellow servants' sins against us."[152] Jesus combines these two paths in his prayer, "Forgive us the wrong we have done as we forgive those who wrong us" (Matt 6:12).

"Do you want to know of a third path?" St. John Chrysostom asks. "It consists of prayer that is fervent, careful and comes from the heart."[153] Again, Chrysostom echoes Jesus' invitation: "Ask, and you will receive. Seek, and you will find. Knock, and it will be opened to you" (Matt 7:7).

"If you want to hear of a fourth," Chrysostom continues, "I will mention almsgiving, whose power is great and far-reaching. . . . The widow proved that when she put her two mites into the box!"[154]

For a final path to repentance, St. John Chrysostom points to humility: "If [one] lives a modest, humble life, that no less than the other things I have mentioned, takes sin away. . . . The tax collector who had no good deeds to mention . . . offered his humility instead and was relieved of a heavy burden of sins."[155]

Like the title of a song, repentance is "a many splendored thing."

QUESTION FOR YOUR REFLECTION

Which of these five paths to repentance disturbs your conscience?

WEDNESDAY

WORD

"Two evils have my people done:
*   they have forsaken me, the source of living waters;*
They have dug themselves cisterns,
*   broken cisterns, that hold no water"* (Jer 2:13).

REFLECTION

Two longings vie for attention. The needs of earthly residence compete with humanity's thirst to share communion with God and God's saints forever. If choice leads only to the satisfaction of this world's cravings, it digs "broken cisterns that hold no water." But if choice leads to Christ, we deliver ourselves over to a thirst that silences all others.

St. Columban writes, "Let us drink from [Christ], as from a fountain, with an abundance of love. May we drink him with the fullness of desire, and may we take pleasure in his sweetness and savor" (St. Columban, abbot).[156]

Life after death is eternal because the desire to drink from the fountain of Christ's love is unquenchable. That is why Jesus still cries out, "If anyone thirsts, . . . come to me; . . . let him drink . . ." (John 7:37).

QUESTION FOR YOUR REFLECTION

Recalling the image of "broken cisterns," why do you think hoarding is futile?

THURSDAY

WORD

"But you have sinned with many lovers,
and yet you would return to me! says the LORD" (Jer 3:1).

REFLECTION

With the wounds of her adulterous life laid bare, Mary Magdalene stands repentant before justice devoid of mercy. She faces despair until the mercy of Jesus challenges her accusers: "Let the man among you who has no sin be the first to cast a stone at her" (John 8:7). When the last of her accusers departs, she follows Jesus for the rest of her life.

In the light of Christ's mercy, we hear Jeremiah speaking the hope of all sinners: "Even though our crimes bear witness against us, take action, O LORD, for the honor of your name—even though our rebellions are many, though we have sinned against you" (Jer 14:7). Hope is nurtured when justice and mercy meet. This meeting is in Christ's assurance to Mary Magdalene: "Nor do I condemn you. You may go. But from now on, avoid this sin" (John 8:11).

The mercy of Jesus awakens in Mary Magdalene a desire for a love that transcends all earthly desires. She discovers that "the more the soul loves, the more it desires to love and the greater [the desire], greater still its healing" (St. Columban, abbot).[157]

QUESTION FOR YOUR REFLECTION

Formerly an adulteress, Mary Magdalene was among the first to whom Christ appeared after his resurrection. What is the "justification" for this appearance?

FRIDAY

WORD

> *"Proclaim it in Judah, . . .*
> *Say, 'Fall in, let us march*
> *to the fortified cities' "* (Jer 4:5).

REFLECTION

Repentant words without repentant deeds are empty. Repentant deeds sound just as empty from hearts not yet rent by God's mercy. "I bid you not to tear your garments but rather to 'rend your hearts' which are laden with sin" (St. Jerome, priest).[158]

When repentant words and deeds are linked to mercy-filled hearts, the repentant become "fortified cities" not likely to yield to forces bent on the destruction of goodness. This goodness—virtue—is at the heart of human worth. Its substance is the presence of Christ, whose mercy has been welcomed into cities "fortified" by repentance.

The publican's prayer, "O God, be merciful to me, a sinner" (Luke 18:13), moves Christ to remark, "Believe me, this man went home from the temple justified" (Luke 18:14).

Repentant words and deeds linked to a broken heart fortify us to be a city of God.

QUESTION FOR YOUR REFLECTION

Someone has suggested that religion means "relinking." In that light, how is repentance an act of religion?

SATURDAY

WORD

> *"Put not your trust in the deceitful words: 'This is the temple of the LORD! . . .' Only if you thoroughly reform your ways and your deeds . . . will I remain with you in this place"* (Jer 7:4-7).

REFLECTION

Evangelization is a passover experience. It takes place when sacrament and word pass over to their lived meaning. St. John Chrysostom writes:

> Do you want to honor Christ's body? Then do not scorn him in his nakedness, nor honor him here in Church with silken garments while neglecting him outside where he is cold and naked. For he who said, "This is my body" and made it so with his words, also said: "You saw me hungry and did not feed me," and "inasmuch as you did not do it for one of these, the least of my brothers [and sisters], you did not do it for me." What we do here in Church requires a pure heart, not special garments; what we do outside requires great dedication (St. John Chrysostom, bishop).[159]

In the passover of word and sacrament to their lived meaning, evangelization is effective. It empowers hearts with love and makes them eager to link chalices made precious with gold to hearts made precious with love.

QUESTION FOR YOUR REFLECTION

Why is evangelization a passover experience?

Twenty-second Week in Ordinary Time

WORD

"Happy are we if we do the deeds of which we have heard and sung. Our hearing them means having them planted in us, while our doing them shows that the seed has borne fruit" (St. Augustine, bishop).[160]

REFLECTION

The illusion of illusions: "God must surely favor me because I have earned everything I need and want." These words suggest that God's favor *follows* from what we have done for God.

St. Augustine warns about this illusion: " 'For we have been saved by [God's] grace,' says the Apostle, 'and not by our works, lest anyone may boast; for it is by his grace that we have been saved.' It is not as if a good life of some sort came first, and that thereupon God showed his love and esteem for it from on high."[161]

When a cripple begs for an alms, Peter responds, "Look at us! . . . I have neither silver nor gold, but what I have I give you! In the name of Jesus Christ the Nazorean, walk" (Acts 3:4, 6). What does Peter "have"? He has only the riches of Christ's wondrous deeds as a sign of his favor. It is no illusion that the cripple walks.

QUESTION FOR YOUR REFLECTION

What we do flows from who we are. How does the life and mission of Jesus confirm this philosopher's axiom?

WORD

"Many hear the world more easily than they hear God; they follow the desires of the flesh more readily than the pleasures of God" (The Imitation of Christ).[162]

REFLECTION

From Scripture's beginnings it is clear that God is the origin of sacredness: "God looked at everything he had made and he found it very good" (Gen 1:31). That God is the origin of sacredness remains constant because faith preserves the perspective that keeps our eyes fixed on goodness beyond this world's perspective of what is good.

When faith is weak, its long-range perspective is exchanged for a perspective of sacredness seen only in the goods of this world. This exchange is easily made by those who equate sovereignty with the individualism that "sanctifies" private choice.

When "sanctity" of private choice determines the beginning and end of human life, the "pleasures of God" will have been exchanged for "the desires of the flesh." No choice is more sacred than God's plan "to bring all things in the heavens and on earth into one under Christ's headship" (Eph 1:10).

QUESTION FOR YOUR REFLECTION

How does "sanctity" of private choice conflict with God as the source of sanctity?

TUESDAY

WORD

"You duped me, O LORD, and I let myself be duped" (Jer 20:7).

REFLECTION

Saints are different! Just as human nature makes a difference to the Son of God, so his divine nature makes a difference to us. It was this difference that caused people to malign Jeremiah and bring him to grieve, "You duped me, O LORD, and I let myself be duped."

The psalmist prays, "I hate men of divided heart, but I love your law" (Ps 119:113). This "law" is God's reason for human life. Every human being exists for a purpose beyond this world's specifications.

God's specifications are different! God creates humanity to be *like* God. All who choose to live wholeheartedly according to this specification live differently from those who choose others.

Saints rejoice at feeling "duped" because Jesus Christ, after crying out on the cross, "My God, my God, why have you forsaken me?" (Matt 27:46), was raised from the dead.

QUESTION FOR YOUR REFLECTION

"The life I live is not my own; Christ is living in me" (Gal 2:20). What difference do these words of St. Paul make in our lives?

WEDNESDAY

WORD

> *"For just as [the] physical body of Christ was crucified and buried, and afterward raised up, so in the same way the whole body of Christ's holy ones has been crucified and lives no longer with its own life"* (Origen, priest).[163]

REFLECTION

Prophets are misunderstood when their words point beyond sacred symbols to their realities. They arouse the anger of people whose sense of sacredness is confined only to symbols. Jesus stirs the people's wrath when he rightly appropriates to himself the sacredness people have assigned to the temple: "Destroy this temple . . . and in three days I will raise it up" (John 2:19).

Jesus is the "temple" that God raised up three days after his earthly body had been destroyed. His resurrection justifies the sacredness of human life, in which Christ continues to invest his divinity. Baptized into Christ's divine presence, "the whole body of Christ's holy ones has been crucified and lives no longer with its own life."

The body of Christ is the Church. It is sacred because it "is a temple of the Holy Spirit" (1 Cor 6:19), who longs to reveal the face of Christ.

QUESTION FOR YOUR REFLECTION

"Whoever is alive and believes in me will never die" (John 11:26). What meaning do these words have beyond their literal meaning?

THURSDAY

WORD

"It might have been unclear to which poor [Jesus] was referring, if after the 'blessed are the poor' he had not added anything about the kind of poor he had in mind. . . . When he says: 'Blessed are the poor in spirit,' he shows that the kingdom of heaven is to be given to those who are distinguished by their humility of soul rather than their lack of worldly goods" (St. Leo the Great, pope).[164]

REFLECTION

Who are those "distinguished by their humility of soul"? They are the ones who share St. Paul's conviction, "I have accounted all else rubbish so that Christ may be my wealth and I may be in him, not having any justice of my own based on observance of the law" (Phil 3:8-9). The humble of soul do not reckon what they possess as their riches; they reckon who they are *in Christ* as their wealth.

The humble of soul acknowledge themselves to be trustees for God's possessions. They regard themselves as stewards, as dispensers of what they legally own but spiritually owe. The humble of soul translate their possessions into compassion for God's least ones. This nobility enables the poor in spirit to discover what it means to be blest. They discover that "the reign of God is theirs" (Matt 5:3).

"The kingdom of heaven is to be given to those who are distinguished by their humility of soul rather than their lack of worldly goods."

QUESTION FOR YOUR REFLECTION

What is the difference between legal ownership and spiritual ownership?

WORD

"You shall be my people, and I will be your God" (Jer 30:22).

REFLECTION

When equality is confined to equal opportunity for this world's riches, the ancient lie continues: "God knows well that the moment you eat of [the fruit of the tree] your eyes will be opened and you will be like gods who know what is good and what is bad" (Gen 3:5).

God defies this allegation when, through Jeremiah, he says, "You shall be my people, and I will be your God." This identity makes both rich and poor equal. We are equal not in what we possess but in who we are. We are like God! This likeness is evidenced by those who generously distribute their possessions to the poor.

St. Leo the Great comments: "[Generosity] is open to all . . ., no matter what their class or condition, because all can be equal in their willingness to give, however unequal they may be in earthly fortunes."[165]

The "narrow gate" (Matt 7:13) is wide for all who approach it in the image and likeness of God's generosity.

QUESTION FOR YOUR REFLECTION

"Life doesn't get any better than this," says a TV commercial. How do commercials like this echo the serpent's lie to Adam and Eve?

WORD

"Set up road markers, put up guideposts" (Jer 31:21).

REFLECTION

When we misunderstand the meaning of Jesus' beatitudes, it may be that we fail to see his linkage between the blessed and their blessings. For example, St. Leo the Great addresses a misunderstanding about those who mourn, and the comfort they shall receive (see Matt 5:4). He contends that the blessed are those who mourn for the sinners who victimize the innocent. "Religious grief," he writes, "mourns for the sin, one's own or another's. . . . Indeed, [whoever] does wrong is more to be lamented than [those] who suffer it."[166]

Those who mourn for sinners are likewise blessed when they see the conversions that become the "markers" and "guideposts" of their tears. St. Augustine, for example, became a consolation for his mother, St. Monica, who spent most of her life in prayers and tears begging God for her son's repentance. Augustine's conversion became a "marker" and "guidepost" not only for his mother but for millions of people who have been moved to repentance by his conversion.

QUESTION FOR YOUR REFLECTION

In the light of St. Leo's comment about those who mourn, how is the Church's opposition to capital punishment justified?

Twenty-third Week in Ordinary Time

SUNDAY

WORD

"In the inexpressible joy of [heaven's] eternal vision, human nature will possess 'what eye has not seen or ear heard,' what man's heart has never conceived" (St. Leo the Great, pope).[167]

REFLECTION

Beatitudes are markers that point out the way to human meaning. They point to the emptiness that becomes consolation. For example:

133

"Blest are they who hunger and thirst for holiness; they shall have their fill" (Matt 5:6). This hunger and thirst reveals hearts that have been emptied of the moorings that fasten us to time.

"Blest are they who show mercy; mercy shall be theirs" (Matt 5:7). Here is a consolation for hearts that have been emptied of a justice rooted in retaliation. Merciful hearts are rich with longings for reconciliation. These longings are realized when mercy inhabits hearts no longer subject to the law of retaliation.

"Blest are the single-hearted for they shall see God" (Matt 5:8). The single-hearted are cleansed of all that prevents them from seeing " 'what eye has not seen or ear heard' [or] . . . heart has never conceived."

Sinners miss the mark of human meaning when they seek only this world's markers and guideposts to consolation.

QUESTION FOR YOUR REFLECTION

In what way are empty feelings signs of God's call to a life of blessedness even here on earth?

MONDAY

WORD

"Remain quietly in this land . . . for I am with you to save you" (Jer 42:10-11).

REFLECTION

In the pursuit of lasting peace, the "land" on which we are commanded to "remain" is God's will. This is the soil into which God asks that we sink the roots of our willfulness. Obedience to the command to "remain quietly in this land" puts us on the land of peace destined to be our home forever.

St. Leo the Great writes, "Even the most intimate bonds of friendship and the closest affinity of minds cannot truly lay claim to peace if they are not in agreement with the will of God."[168]

The sincerity of praying "your will be done" (Matt 6:10) is tested against our sincerity of being instruments of peace. Peacemakers understand the meaning of being sons and daughters of God when God's will is their lifetime pursuit. Jesus says, "Whoever does the will of God is brother and sister and mother to me" (Mark 3:35). It is in the light of that kinship that he declares, "Blest too the peacemakers; they shall be called sons of God" (Matt 5:9).

QUESTION FOR YOUR REFLECTION

Jesus says, " 'Peace' is my farewell to you, my peace is my gift to you" (John 14:27). What is the "peace" of Christ?

TUESDAY

WORD

"I will stand at my guard post,
and station myself upon the rampart,
And keep watch to see what he will say to me,
and what answer he will give to my complaint" (Heb 2:1).

REFLECTION

Happiness is realized when we take a stand on the beatitudes of Jesus. The word "stand" is appropriate because persecution is the price of Christ's peace. "Blest are those persecuted for holiness' sake; the reign of God is theirs" (Matt 5:10). The reward for this last beatitude is the same as for the first: "How blest are the poor in spirit; the reign of God is theirs" (Matt 5:3).

From beginning to end, poverty makes straight the way to discipleship. Bereft of this world's instruments of war as the way to peace, "the poor" are filled with the presence of the Prince of Peace. Nevertheless, Christ's followers are mocked and persecuted for their stand on "the rampart[s]" of peace.

Yet the followers of Christ are happy, because their stand emboldens them to "keep watch to see what he will say to [them]." Christ's answer from beginning to end remains, "The reign of God is theirs."

QUESTION FOR YOUR REFLECTION

How is faithful Eucharistic assembly a sign of our stand on God's Word, "I myself am the living bread come down from heaven" (John 6:51)?

WEDNESDAY

WORD

"Let us take our stand on secure ground [that we might] see what [God] is saying to us and what reply we ought to make to his charge" (St. Bernard, abbot).[169]

REFLECTION

The heresy of Jansenism, though condemned, left us with an utterly disfigured humility. Jansenism persuaded people to believe that they were unworthy of God and that humility was distance from God. Humility is disfigured when people disbelieve "I am with you always, until the end of the world" (Matt 28:20).

Humility is genuine when it moves us to "take a stand on [the] secure ground" of our *worth* in the eyes of God. We are worthy of God when humility fixes our eyes on the purpose for which God created us, a purpose that causes Jesus to be with us "until the end of the world." Humility is genuine when we believe that we have been created in the likeness of God. That's our worth!

Jesus reveals human worth not by keeping his distance but by embracing our sinful humanity. When we believe that we are so embraced, humility configures us to Jesus Christ.

QUESTION FOR YOUR REFLECTION

What is the "stand" that keeps humility on "secure ground"?

WORD

"When [the psalmist] says 'blessed' all 'who dwell in your house,' he means that they enjoy as much happiness as can be conceived" (St. Bruno, priest).[170]

REFLECTION

The beatitudes are concrete answers to St. Bruno's question, "Does God really help us [in our journey toward] life?"[171] Jesus begins each beatitude with "blessed" to signify that in him the poor in spirit experience the gift of God's happiness here upon earth. He cites the beatitudes as reasons for following him and his "way" of being open to "as much happiness as can be conceived."

Those who say they want to follow Christ must be open to his way of experiencing beatitude. This "way" is the world's "less traveled road."[172] It is a peace that travels the way of poverty in spirit, sorrow, humility, hunger and thirst for holiness' sake, mercy, single-heartedness, peacemaking, and persecution. To be like Christ in these circumstances is to be at home with him and truly blessed in him.

QUESTION FOR YOUR REFLECTION

We speak of Eucharist as Holy Communion. How do the beatitudes point out ways of living a life of holy communion?

WORD

"The Lord's rejection does not last forever" (Lam 3:31).

REFLECTION

Our longing to be forgiven pales before God's longing to forgive. No sinfulness exiles us from God's watchfulness for signs of remorse and return. "While he was still a long way off, his father caught sight of him and was deeply moved" (Luke 15:20).

Jesus is one with us so that these two longings might be wedded. He possesses divinity's longing to forgive and is eager to be united with humanity's longing to be forgiven. With this union both God and humankind are no longer "a long way off."

The wedding of these two longings is the blessing of sacramental forgiveness. It is the blessing that unites sinless Christ with his Church longing for sinlessness. Such union is why Jesus continues to rejoice sacramentally: "Let us eat and celebrate because this son of mine was dead and has come back to life" (Luke 15:23-24).

"The Church is incapable of forgiving any sin without Christ, and Christ is unwilling to forgive any sin without the Church. . . . 'What God has joined together man must not separate.' This is a great mystery, but I understand it as referring to Christ and the Church" (Blessed Isaac of Stella, abbot).[173]

QUESTION FOR YOUR REFLECTION

How is the sacrament of matrimony echoed in the sacrament of reconciliation?

SATURDAY

WORD

"The Word of the all-good Father . . . restored by his power all that belongs to [humanity's] estate" (St. Athanasius, bishop).[174]

REFLECTION

The mind is numbed at God's patience. God bears the insult of being traded for a trinket of perishability. Choosing the tree's alleged God-likeness, humanity's parents disowned their destiny to bear the fruit of God's very own image and likeness. God's patience, however, "restored . . . all that belongs to [humanity's] estate." Jesus Christ chose the tree that gives humankind the power to reown the destiny that Adam and Eve disowned in the garden of Eden.

Jesus spent his entire earthly life disowning the illusion that this world's images of happiness are worth more than the wholeness of heart, soul, mind, and strength by which he defined his commandments of love. His lifetime of reowning—redeeming—us climaxed on the cross when nothing of this world's goods rescued him. Jesus died on the cross "for all so that those who live might live no longer for themselves, but for him who for their sakes died and was raised up" (2 Cor 5:15).

QUESTION FOR YOUR REFLECTION

Mortal sin flows from a mortal attitude. What is that attitude?

Twenty-fourth Week in Ordinary Time

SUNDAY

WORD

"Above the firmament over their heads something like a throne could be seen, looking like sapphire. Upon it was seated, up above, one who had the appearance of a man" (Ezek 1:26).

REFLECTION

While exiled in Babylon, the priest Ezekiel receives a call from God to exercise prophetic leadership. From the moment of that call, not a shred of doubt lingers about his people's future. He had seen the presence of God, "who had the appearance of a man" with a light that surrounded the earth "like the bow which appears in the clouds on a rainy day" (Ezek 1:28).

Ezekiel sees the point! The people are not abandoned. This vision expresses the certainty that defines hope. This hope becomes his command to be the shepherd of exiles, a mandate Jesus was to bring to the exiles of the whole world. "I am the good shepherd. I know my sheep and my sheep know me . . .; for these sheep I will give my life" (John 10:14-15).

St. Augustine challenges pastors to be images of the "Good Shepherd," a challenge he daily applies to himself: "I am a Christian [and] I am a leader. I am a Christian for my sake whereas I am a leader for your sake; the fact that I am a Christian is to my own advantage; but I am a leader for your advantage" (St. Augustine, bishop).[175] This is the leadership that gathers all men and women to Christ, the Good Shepherd.

QUESTION FOR YOUR REFLECTION

How is the association of priesthood with "shepherd" evidence that the words "gathering" and "Church" are synonymous?

MONDAY

WORD

"[The Lord] said to me: Son of man, eat what is before you; eat this scroll, then go, speak to the house of Israel" (Ezek 3:1).

REFLECTION

The words "celebration of the Eucharist" express the union of God's word heard and God's word lived. When Christians become the word they have heard, they understand the link of Eucharist and celebration.

The union of word and sacrament form God's people into a communion of God and humankind. Such formation reveals the power of God's Word enfleshed in all who have decided to become sacraments of God's presence. This witness is the meaning Pope Paul VI gives to evangelization: "For the Church, the first means of evangelization is the witness of an authentically Christian life, given over to God in a communion that nothing should destroy and at the same time given to one's neighbor with limitless zeal."[176]

Our challenge to become what we celebrate resonates with God's call to Ezekiel: "Eat this scroll, then go, speak to the house of Israel."

QUESTION FOR YOUR REFLECTION

How are the words "eat this scroll" linked to Eucharistic communion?

TUESDAY

WORD

"Let [God's shepherds] not seek any benefit for themselves . . ., rather, let them provide the light of the true word for the sake of [people's] enlightenment" (St. Augustine, bishop).[177]

REFLECTION

Brought "into the inner court of the LORD's house, and there at the door of the LORD's temple" the Lord shows Ezekiel twenty-five priestly shepherds with their backs to the temple "bowing down to the sun" (Ezek 8:16). This is the "greater abomination" (see Ezek 8:15) that towers over all others in the temple.

These shepherds, commissioned to lead God's people to the "LORD's house" filled with light greater than a trillion suns, have acted abominably. They have severed themselves from faith in God's presence and its link to God's light. Their idolatry has left the people in darkness.

Jesus is the "Sun of Justice" (see Mal 3:20) for shepherds called to lead God's people to the light of justice. This light, contends St. Augustine, radiates from shepherds who "seek no benefit for themselves, lest they appear to be preaching the gospel for the sake of their own need and privation."[178] Such shepherds are rays of the "Sun of Justice."

To his shepherds Jesus says, "You are the light of the world. . . . Your light must shine before men so that they may see goodness in your acts and give praise to your heavenly Father" (Matt 5:14, 16).

QUESTION FOR YOUR REFLECTION

Why is consumerism an "abomination"?

WEDNESDAY

WORD

"I will restore to you the land of Israel. They shall return to it and remove from it all its detestable abominations" (Ezek 11:17-18).

REFLECTION

For the "abomination" of idolatry, the chosen people become exiles. Nevertheless, God sends Ezekiel with the promise of restored honor: "I will gather you from the nations and assemble you from the countries over which you have been scattered, and I will restore you to the land of Israel" (Ezek 11:17).

That promise is fully kept as Jesus inhabits humankind's exile. He comes not only as the "Sun of Justice" (see Mal 3:20) but also as the temple radiating the fullness of God's light. Throughout his public ministry Jesus witnesses the idolatry of other shepherds bowing before the spurious light of law. Deeply hurt by this "abomination" he cries, "O Jerusalem, Jerusalem . . . ! How often have I yearned to gather your children, as a mother bird gathers her young under her wings, but you refused me. Recall the saying, 'You will find your temple deserted'" (Matt 23:37-38).

The Church is God's "land" where priestly shepherds gather people from all nations to be the temple of that land. The glory of God fills this temple and becomes visible in the lives of priests and people honored to be the temple of God's "land."

QUESTION FOR YOUR REFLECTION

Current advertising describes many products as "ultimate." What is abominable about this?

WORD

"The word of the LORD came to [Ezekiel]: Son of man, you live in the midst of a rebellious house" (Ezek 12:1).

REFLECTION

Long before Christ, God grieved for the "rebellious house" whose idolatrous shepherds had, in effect, said to their flocks, "Get lost!" As exiles, the "lost" pray:

> By the streams of Babylon
>   we sat and wept . . .
> If I forget you, Jerusalem,
>   may my right hand be forgotten! (Ps 137:1, 5).

St. Augustine speaks severely of shepherds whose self-indulgence turns them into "a rebellious house." "Even the strong sheep . . . begins to say in his heart, 'If my pastor lives like that, why should I not live like him?' . . . The shepherd who lives a wicked life before the people kills the sheep under his care. Let not such a shepherd deceive himself because the sheep is not dead, for though it still lives, he is a murderer.[179]

Jesus' parable of the lost sheep and the loving care of their searching shepherd sounds the depths of God's longing to build a house where a communion of hearts is bonded by love. This is the house where God longs to exclaim, "Son of man, you live in a house of love."

QUESTION FOR YOUR REFLECTION

If religion bonds us to God and one another, what is the bond?

WORD

"Lift him up from the sand and put him on the rock. Let him be in Christ, if you wish him to be a Christian. Let him turn his thoughts to sufferings" (St. Augustine, bishop).[180]

REFLECTION

St. Paul begins his Second Letter to the Corinthians with encouragement: "He comforts us in all our afflictions" (2 Cor 1:4). St. Paul is encouraging because he names affliction as the instrument through which God comforts us.

St. Augustine takes no comfort from shepherds who promise this world's comfort to all who seek holiness. "God . . . made no such promise to this world. On the contrary, God foretold hardship upon hardship in this world until the end of time. And [shepherds] want the Christian to be exempt from these troubles? Precisely because he is a Christian, he is destined to suffer more in this world."[181]

The test of life in Christ is the willingness to journey "in all our afflictions." Sufferings are not barriers that entice shepherds to lead their flocks on detours around them. Good shepherds remain on the road of afflictions so that the followers of Christ might possess God's comforts "in all [their] afflictions." Detours annoy, but the comforts that sufferings possess fill us with the courage of which David sings:

> Even though I walk in the dark valley
> I fear no evil; for you are at my side
> With your rod and your staff
> that give me courage (Ps 23:4).

QUESTION FOR YOUR REFLECTION

God "comforts us in all our afflictions." Why are these encouraging words?

SATURDAY

WORD

"It is not that temptations will be lacking, but that God will not permit anyone to be tempted beyond what he can bear" (St. Augustine, bishop).[182]

REFLECTION

The proof that we live in Christ is not the disappearance of temptation. Rather, it is the appearance of courage, which mirrors Christ's

144

response to temptation at the beginning of his public ministry. Jesus is led "into the desert by the Spirit to be tempted by the devil" (Matt 4:1).

He acknowledges that he is not exempt from temptation. By this action he clearly states that before he calls all men and women to live in him he must, except for sin, live fully in them.

The basis of every temptation is the illusion that this world's comforts are the substance of human purpose. Every temptation suggests that we are both in the world and *of* the world. Christ confronts the enticement of that illusion so that its lie might be exposed. He allows himself to be tempted so that we may understand that Christ is both in us and of us. He is fully human that we might be wholly divine.

Christ's fidelity in the face of temptation occasions St. Paul's exhortation: "Do not conform yourselves to this age but be transformed by the renewal of your mind, so that you may judge what is God's will, what is good, pleasing and perfect" (Rom 12:2).

QUESTION FOR YOUR REFLECTION

When people fall for the illusion that they are of this world, they are susceptible to the agony of depression. Why?

Twenty-fifth Week in Ordinary Time

SUNDAY

WORD

"Reveal . . . what is hidden, and thus you will open the roof and lower the paralytic to the feet of Christ" (St. Augustine, bishop).[183]

REFLECTION

A common complaint: "I feel helpless before the media's daily barrage of war, hunger, and oppression; I feel paralyzed."

One cannot dispute the media's role as dispensers of bad news. One can dispute bad news as the cause of feeling paralyzed. No such feeling surfaces when our lives are completely open at the feet of Jesus Christ. "Reveal . . . what is hidden," St. Augustine writes, "and thus you will open the roof and lower the paralytic to the feet of Christ."

Jesus does not gaze on bad news. He gazes on the faith that moves us to "reveal . . . what is hidden" at the feet of Christ's sacrament of forgiveness. His gazes on shepherds whose priestly ministry carries their flocks "to the feet of Christ." When Jesus sees such faith, he speaks good news: "Stand up! Pick up your mat and go home" (Mark 2:11).

QUESTION FOR YOUR REFLECTION

Jesus healed the paralysis of sin before he healed the paralysis of limb. What does this procedure say?

MONDAY

WORD

"I will rescue them from every place where they were scattered. . . . I will bring them back to their own country" (Ezek 34:12-13).

REFLECTION

Before his passion on the cross, Jesus experiences a passion in his heart: "I pray . . . that all may be one as you, Father, are in me, and I in you; I pray that they may be [one] in us; . . . that their unity may be complete; . . . so shall the world know, . . . that you loved them as you loved me" (John 17:20-21, 23).

"That all may be one." These words speak of Christ's longing to gather all peoples into the homeland of his Father's identity. They speak of the Church's identity and its mission to "go . . . and make disciples of all the nations. Baptize them in the name 'of the Father, and of the Son, and of the Holy Spirit' " (Matt 28:19).

Christ's heartfelt passion is echoed in the heart of St. Augustine: "I shall recall the straying; I shall seek the lost. Whether they wish it or not, I shall do it. . . . So far as God whom I fear grants me the strength, I shall search everywhere."[184]

QUESTION FOR YOUR REFLECTION

The word "church" means "assembly." What is the mission significance of the word "catholic?"

TUESDAY

WORD

"Which shepherds are dead? Those who seek what is theirs and not what is Christ's" (St. Augustine, bishop).[185]

REFLECTION

When priestly shepherds promise obedience to bishops they acknowledge a mission to link themselves to the Church's mission of responding to Christ's prayer "that all may be one" (John 17:21).

Obedience is authentic when it springs from listening hearts. It is of such hearts that God speaks to Ezekiel: "I will give you a new heart and place a new spirit within you, taking from your bodies your stony hearts and giving you natural hearts" (Ezek 36:26).

"New hearts" listen to God's Spirit longing to gather all nations; "stony hearts" listen only to themselves. "New hearts" are alive because they seek "what is Christ's." "Stony hearts" are dead because they seek only for themselves. What is of Christ is forever alive; what is of self perishes.

At no time are shepherds more *ecclesial* than when they are obedient. In obedience they listen to Christ's universal plea sounding in their listening hearts: "Go into the whole world and proclaim the good news to all creation" (Mark 16:15). "Good news"? Yes! "That all may be one."

QUESTION FOR YOUR REFLECTION

How is the obedience of priestly shepherds and priestly people linked to the reason for the Church's existence?

WORD

"The hand of the LORD came upon me, and he led me out in the spirit of the LORD and set me in the center of the plain, which was now filled with bones" (Ezek 37:1).

REFLECTION

Obedience that merely implements laws is really subservience. This charade blocks God's Spirit from transforming "the plain . . . filled with bones." Obedience makes way for God's Spirit to crush "stony hearts" and transform them into hearts "natural" to God's communion of persons (see Ezek 36:26).

The obedience that takes to heart God's imperatives is the heart of God's Trinitarian life. This is the heart that gives life to the "dry bones" of the spiritless for whom law is "the center of the plain." Mary's obedient heart united Jesus with our humanity. It was from her that the "dry bones" of humanity were given the "new heart" of Jesus her Son. That new heart springs from the obedience that moves Jesus to acknowledge:

I do nothing by myself.
I say only what the Father has taught me.
The One who sent me is with me.
He has not deserted me
since I always do what pleases him (John 8:28-29).

QUESTION FOR YOUR REFLECTION

What is the difference between obedience and subservience?

WORD

"I will take the Israelites from among the nations to which they have come, and gather them from all sides to bring them back to their land. I will make them one nation upon the land, in the mountains of Israel, and there shall be one prince for them all" (Ezek 37:21-22).

REFLECTION

The collapse of communism in Eastern Europe reveals the hollowness of allegations that associate unity with economic security. In a matter of days millions of people gathered, convinced that such unity is a lie. It is apparent that they responded to "the timeless," which God "has put . . . into their hearts" (Eccl 3:11). This is the "timeless" that gathers all nations into the unity of God's "I am."

The Son of God, clothed with humanity's flesh, never ceases to gather nations "upon the land" of communion with God and one another. This communion is the "land" into which Jesus sows the message that yields "a hundred- or sixty- or thirtyfold" harvest of peace (Matt 13:23).

Ezekiel speaks for "the timeless": "I will make with them a covenant of peace; it shall be an everlasting covenant . . . and I will multiply them, and put my sanctuary among them forever. My dwelling shall be with them; I will be their God, and they shall be my people. Thus the nations shall know that it is I, the LORD, who make Israel holy, when my sanctuary shall be set up among them forever" (Ezek 37:26-28).

QUESTION FOR YOUR REFLECTION

What is the difference between unity and uniformity?

WORD

> *" 'My sheep,' he says, 'hear my voice and follow me.' In this statement I find that all good shepherds are one in the one shepherd"* (St. Augustine, bishop).[186]

REFLECTION

Unity is one of the Church's four marks. This mark is not the uniformity that rightly provides order for the common understandings that facilitate unity. Unity is the mark of the communion that reveals Christ's way, truth, and life, revealing that "all good shepherds are one in the one shepherd." This is the communion that Jesus continually asks to be renewed at each Eucharist: "This is my body to be given for you. Do this as a remembrance of me" (Luke 22:19).

Sacramental Communion is a beautiful moment! It signifies a solidarity of shepherd and flock dedicated to the obedience of Christ's plea, "Do this as a remembrance of me." Truly, Christ is *re-membered* when both shepherd and flock acknowledge and fulfill their baptismal commitment to be likenesses of Christ's communion with both Father and Spirit. The common vocation of shepherds and flocks is to become the communion that they celebrate.

QUESTION FOR YOUR REFLECTION

Good flocks mirror good shepherds. Why do good shepherds also mirror good flocks?

WORD

"I saw water flowing from beneath the threshold of the temple toward the east. . . . Wherever this water flows, every sort of living creature that can multiply shall live" (Ezek 47:1, 9).

REFLECTION

From Minnesota's Lake Itasca, a trickle of water begins the mighty Mississippi River. For hundreds of miles this tiny stream gathers to itself countless brooks and rivers from America's midwest interior. When it ends it resembles the gulf into which it enters.

The Mississippi's journey from stream to gulf is a parable of Christ and his Church. From "I am the good shepherd" (John 10:14) until his return in Spirit to cover the whole world, Jesus never ceases to be "a fountain within him, leaping up to provide eternal life" (John 4:14).

St. Hilary speaks of this marvel: "The river of God is brimming with water; that is to say, we are inundated by the gifts of the Holy Spirit and from that fountain of life the river of God pours into us in full flood" (St. Hilary, bishop).[187]

The Church is the temple of Ezekiel's vision: "I saw water flowing from beneath the threshold of the temple toward the east. . . . Wherever this water flows, every[thing] . . . shall live." The Church's union with Christ the Good Shepherd allows her to claim:

The LORD is my shepherd; I shall not want.
    In verdant pastures he gives me repose;
Beside restful waters he leads me;
    he refreshes my soul (Ps 23:1-3).

QUESTION FOR YOUR REFLECTION

The Church is both a tiny stream and a mighty river. How has this been true in your life?

Twenty-sixth Week in Ordinary Time

WORD

"I . . . entertain . . . expectations in your regard since I hold all of you dear—you who, to a man, are sharers of my gracious lot when I lie in prison or am summoned to defend the solid grounds on which the gospel rests" (Phil 1:7).

REFLECTION

No encouragement is more uplifting than to know the expectations others have of us. St. Paul offers such encouragement to the Philippians, whose faith inspired him to state unconditionally, "He who has begun the good work in you will carry it through to completion, right up to the day of Christ Jesus" (Phil 1:6).

St. Paul entertains the expectations Jesus has for all of us: "Love one another. . . . As my love has been for you, so must your love be for each other" (John 13:34). These words are astonishing! He *expects* us to love each other *as* he loves us! Jesus expects us to love as he loves because we have been created in the likeness of God. "God is love" (1 John 4:16), and our likeness to that love merits Christ's astonishing expectations that we love one another as he unfailingly loves us.

St. Polycarp also addresses encouraging words to the Philippians: "I rejoice with you greatly in the Lord Jesus Christ because you have assumed the pattern of true love and have rightly helped on their way those who were in chains" (St. Polycarp, bishop and martyr).[188]

QUESTION FOR YOUR REFLECTION

What expectation from another encouraged you to see qualities that you little surmised about yourself?

WORD

'I have full confidence that now as always Christ will be exalted through me, whether I live or die. For, to me, 'life' means Christ; hence dying is so much gain" (Phil 1:20-21).

REFLECTION

"Your father will not be dead as long as you are alive," my mother expressed to me long after my father's death.

Her expression was not hyperbole because we share a solidarity of life with people whose lives have had meaning for us. This solidarity is a communion so intimate that we appropriate to ourselves the characteristics of others. We become like them, a likeness that survives them.

This feature of human life is at the heart of St. Paul's spirituality. His reason for "life" is Jesus Christ, and he does not hedge about his reason for existence: " 'Life' means Christ." So intense is this conviction that, for him, death is not a loss. He feels free to live even while chained in prison. It is from his chains, as from the cross of Jesus, that the message of liberation reaches out to the whole world.

All for whom " 'life' means Christ" are in solidarity with the risen Christ.

QUESTION FOR YOUR REFLECTION

After saying, " 'life' means Christ," St. Paul continues, "hence dying is so much gain." What is this "gain" in light of daily dyings—afflictions, disappointments, persecutions, insults, and the like?

WORD

"It is your special privilege to take Christ's part—not only to believe in him but also to suffer for him" (Phil 1:29).

REFLECTION

On the day of his ascension, Jesus instructed his disciples to "make disciples of all the nations" (Matt 28:19).

St. Peter knew well the standard Jesus expects of discipleship. He remembered him saying that he must "suffer much, be rejected by the elders, the chief priests, and the scribes, be put to death . . . " (Mark 8:31). St. Peter also remembered the reprimand that followed his objection to Jesus' suffering and death: "Get out of my sight, you satan! You are not judging by God's standards but by man's!" (Mark 8:33).

"God's standards" of discipleship call for attitudes that this world rejects. St. Paul writes: "Your attitude must be that of Christ" (Phil 2:5). He states that attitude when he says that Jesus "emptied himself and took . . . the likeness of men . . . obediently accepting even death, death on a cross!" (Phil 2:7-8).

To believe in Christ without accepting affliction is a standard that does not qualify for discipleship. "It is your special privilege to take Christ's part—not only to believe in him but also *to suffer for him*" (emphasis mine).

QUESTION FOR YOUR REFLECTION

How does suffering afford us the opportunity to develop the "attitude" of Christ's standard of discipleship?

WEDNESDAY

WORD

> *"Follow the Lord's example. . . . Show the Lord's own gentleness in your dealings with one another"* (St. Polycarp, bishop and martyr).[189]

REFLECTION

Our love for Christ is genuine if our lives show evidence of daily service to the Word. This service is the substance of discipleship, revealing lives stamped with the identity of Christ.

St. Paul is adamant; the gospel is a way of living for all who have welcomed Christ's identity into their lives. "In everything you do," he writes to the Philippians, "act without grumbling or arguing; prove yourselves innocent and straightforward, children of God beyond reproach in the midst of a twisted and depraved generation—among whom you shine like the stars in the sky while holding fast to the word of life" (Phil 2:14-16).

For St. Paul, "word" and "life" are one. Those who serve the Word of God reflect genuine love in their lives. Those who "show the Lord's own gentleness" follow the gentle command of Jesus: "As I have done, so you must do" (John 13:15). All who live this command are disciples.

QUESTION FOR YOUR REFLECTION

How is the Good Samaritan parable an illustration depicting "word" and "life" as one?

THURSDAY

WORD

"Those things I used to consider gain I have now reappraised as loss in the light of Christ" (Phil 3:7).

REFLECTION

I saw the movie *Citizen Kane* over fifty years ago. Not until the last scene did I see its meaning. It depicts a huge bonfire consuming Citizen Kane's mountain of possessions. As the movie ends the camera closes in on a sled marked "Rosebud" perishing with everything else. Rosebud had been Kane's only possession when he left parents who had sold him to a man of immense wealth.

Citizen Kane follows the well-traveled road of many who pursue wealth. The road takes him to wealth's mountaintop, where he reigns alone. When he dies, Rosebud burns along with his mountain of possessions. Its ashes eloquently speak Christ's words, "What profit does a man show who gains the whole world and destroys himself in the process?" (Mark 8:36).

155

Kane's Rosebud never bloomed. Just as child Kane was traded for money, so Citizen Kane trades his own life for wealth. This is the wealth that consumes the Rosebud, which has failed to flower.

St. Paul discovers his "Rosebud" when Christ appears to him on the way to Damascus. When he later asserts, "I have accounted all else rubbish so that Christ may be my wealth" (Phil 3:8), his Rosebud blooms.

QUESTION FOR YOUR REFLECTION

How does St. Paul's reappraisal of "gain" speak to the necessity of reappraisal in our own lives?

FRIDAY

WORD

> *"As you well know, we have our citizenship in heaven"*
> (Phil 3:20).

REFLECTION

Those who travel abroad guard their passport more closely than any other possession. They "well know" that passports verify citizenship in homelands all over the world, assuring reentry to the lands of their departure.

St. Paul is not unaware of his "citizenship" requirements. Writing to the Corinthians, he says, "What anyone else dares to claim . . . I, too, will dare. Are they Hebrews? So am I! Are they Israelites? So am I! Are they the seed of Abraham? So am I! Are they ministers of Christ? . . . I am more" (2 Cor 11:21-23).

What is the "more" that St. Paul claims as his "citizenship"? In his letter to the Philippians he writes, "He will give a new form to this lowly body of ours and remake it according to the pattern of his glorified body, by his power to subject everything to himself" (Phil 3:21). This "new form" is Christ's identity sealed on ours. It is the "passport" of St. Paul's claim, "I am more."

While we journey in the foreign land of this world we are exhorted to keep close watch on our "passport." " 'Let your moderation be known to all.' . . . That is to say," writes St. Ambrose, "your holiness of life must be evident, not only in the sight of God, but also in the sight of [all]. It . . . must serve also as a memorial of goodness before God and men.[190]

QUESTION FOR YOUR REFLECTION

Why does "I am more" qualify us for heaven's "citizenship" rather than "I own more"?

SATURDAY

WORD

"If you try to outdo one another in showing respect, your life on earth will be that of the angels" (St. Gregory of Nyssa, bishop).[191]

REFLECTION

Lucifer's "I will not serve" stands as the depth of disrespect. It strikes a fatal blow to angelic existence because angels exist for the service of proclaiming the light of God.

Lucifer's condemnation does not call us to be angels but to be temporary creatures of this earth called to the service that befits our creaturehood. We are chosen to reveal the light of God in the creaturehood of our humanity. But like the angels, we have been chosen to render the service of love, which respects one another as a loving God respects us.

Saints like Paul, Polycarp, Ambrose, and Gregory of Nyssa choose the Philippians as models of respectful service. It is to them that St. Gregory asserts, "If you try to outdo one another in showing respect, your life on earth will be like that of the angels." The Philippians choose to serve in the light of God's Word and the tradition of their lived experience in Christ.

QUESTION FOR YOUR REFLECTION

Jesus refers to himself as "light" and "servant." What is the service that unites these two words in him?

Twenty-seventh Week in Ordinary Time

WORD

"May grace, mercy, and peace be yours from God the Father and Christ Jesus our Lord" (1 Tim 1:2).

REFLECTION

The order in which St. Paul places "grace, mercy, and peace" is instructive. His arrangement of these three blessings suggests that we question the order of "law and order."

In the mind of St. Paul, God rules by the law of love. First and foremost, God's grace disposes us to embrace "the love that springs from a pure heart, a good conscience, and sincere faith" (1 Tim 1:5). Grace—rather than law—orders life because it enlightens us to recognize who we *are* and why God loves us. We are loved by God not to be practitioners of endless laws but to be witnesses of God's law of love.

For St. Paul, all blessings flow from envelopment in the grace that empowers us to show mercy and be at peace. He says, "The grace of our Lord has been granted me in overflowing measure, along with . . . faith and love. . . . Christ Jesus came into the world to save sinners" (1 Tim 1:14-15). With this "overflowing measure" we are bound to be at peace.

QUESTION FOR YOUR REFLECTION

Why is law before order questionable?

WORD

"God is one. One also is the mediator between God and men, the man Christ Jesus, who gave himself as a ransom for all" (1 Tim 2:5-6).

REFLECTION

"Kitty, take me home!" was my grandmother's daily plea in the home where she had lived for sixty years. Her exile in the land of senility had betrayed her into believing that she was not at home.

There are evidences of such exile in the way we pray. We are not at home with a prayer that must first travel beyond stars and planets in order to reach God. That is not how St. Paul envisions God's presence. He sees God at home with us: "He had to become like his brothers in every way" (Heb 2:17) so that he might show them compassion.

God is at home with all of us because Jesus is in our midst to bridge heaven and earth. He teaches us to pray, "Your kingdom come, your will be done on earth as it is in heaven" (Matt 6:10). It is God's will, then, that our prayer share room with Christ, who dwells within us. "This room of prayer," St. Ambrose writes, "is always with you, wherever you are, and it is always a secret room, where only God can see you" (St. Ambrose, bishop).[192]

QUESTION FOR YOUR REFLECTION

If God seems far away, who moved?

TUESDAY

WORD

"Wonderful, indeed, is the mystery of our faith" (1 Tim 3:16).

REFLECTION

I asked my third-grade teacher why islands don't float around. Mirthfully she replied, "Oh! that's a mystery."

At age nine this answer might have sufficed. I am grateful, however, that she pursued my question. "Islands don't float," she explained, "because the island you see is the top of the mountain, which the ocean keeps hidden." She added, "That's what mystery means!"

159

"God is one" (1 Tim 2:5), exclaims St. Paul. This oneness is mystery because even though "He was manifested in the flesh, vindicated in the Spirit; seen by the angels; preached among the Gentiles, believed in throughout the world, taken up into glory" (1 Tim 3:16), still, "eye has not seen, ear has not heard, nor has it so much as dawned on man what God has prepared for those who love him" (1 Cor 2:9).

"Wonderful, indeed, is the mystery of our faith."

QUESTION FOR YOUR REFLECTION

Mystery is hiddenness seeking to be revealed. What is the role of faith in this pursuit?

WEDNESDAY

WORD

"The chains which I wear for the sake of Jesus Christ . . . are my plea" (St. Ignatius of Antioch, bishop and martyr).[193]

REFLECTION

My bishop's nineteen-year tenure ended one morning when he suffered a massive stroke. During a conversation with him many days later, I lamented the abruptness that ended his ministry. With warm censure the bishop replied, "My suffering is my ministry." With those simple words he spanned almost nineteen centuries to link himself with St. Ignatius: "The chains which I wear for the sake of Jesus Christ . . . are my plea."

From the hearts of these two bishops come words of censure for all who regard suffering as futile. This is not the mind of Christ, who says, "The hour has come for the Son of Man to be glorified. . . . My soul is troubled now, yet what should I say—Father, save me from this hour? But it was for this that I came to this hour. Father, glorify your name" (John 12:23, 27).

St. Paul welcomes suffering as his ministry to Christ's continuous suffering in the Church, his earthly body: "In my own flesh I fill up what

160

is lacking in the sufferings of Christ for the sake of his body the Church" (Col 1:24). It was "for the sake of [Christ's] body" that my bishop said, "Suffering is my ministry."

QUESTION FOR YOUR REFLECTION

What is "lacking" in Christ's sufferings?

THURSDAY

WORD

"Honor the claims of widows who are real widows—that is, who are alone and bereft" (1 Tim 5:3).

REFLECTION

According to St. Paul, the "real widow, left destitute, is one who has set her hope on God and continues night and day in supplications and prayers" (1 Tim 5:5). Although she has transferred her nuptial union to Christ her spouse, she is made unhappy by the failure of her family to rescue her from the destitution of being "alone and bereft." So imperative is this rescue that "If anyone does not provide for his own relatives, . . . he has denied the faith" (1 Tim 5:8).

Widowhood is symbolic of all who are "alone and bereft." It highlights the necessity of nourishing each person's instinct for the basic security of belonging and being loved. Such security is basic because it is the fulfillment of human purpose—belonging both to God's communion and the communion of the human family.

St. Ignatius of Antioch experiences a sense of widowhood while chained in prison. He loves his people and begs for their loving prayers that they might keep alive the oneness that prison endeavors to disrupt. "I overflow with love for you. . . . Your prayers will perfect me in the eyes of God so that I might yet receive the inheritance promised me by the merciful God" (St. Ignatius of Antioch, bishop and martyr).[194]

QUESTION FOR YOUR REFLECTION

Why is neglect of those who are "alone and bereft" a denial of faith?

161

WORD

"Is there no development of religion in the Church of Christ? Certainly . . . and on the largest scale" (St. Vincent of Lerins, priest).[195]

REFLECTION

I am tempted to say that since my ordination in 1948, the priesthood has changed. The truth is, my understanding of the priesthood has changed. My island perception of priesthood is changing because my understanding of priesthood's mountainous presence is unfolding.

And so it is with the "development of religion." Within understanding's capacity to expand, "development of religion" takes place "on the largest scale." "Tradition which comes from the apostles," write the bishops of the Second Vatican Council, "develops in the Church with the help of the Holy Spirit. For there is a growth in the understanding of the realities and the word which have been handed down."[196]

Development is not the alteration that prevents reality from becoming itself. Development pursues purpose, and when religion's purpose is unfolding, development is having an impact on understanding. "In ancient times," St. Vincent of Lerins observes, "our ancestors sowed the good seed in the harvest field of the Church. . . . There should be no inconsistency between first and last, but we should reap true doctrine from the growth of true teaching, so that when, in the course of time, those first sowings yield an increase it may flourish and be tended in our days also."[197]

QUESTION FOR YOUR REFLECTION

What is the difference between alteration and development?

WORD

"O Timothy, guard what has been committed to you" (1 Tim 6:20).

REFLECTION

St. Paul charges Timothy to carry out a twofold commitment. He asks him to guard not only a flock of people but also the word that is a "two-edged sword" (Heb 4:12) that both hurts and heals. Timothy is charged with the pastoral commitment of bonding his people so that their unity might clearly reveal the body of Christ.

However, in the intimacy that unity secures, there lurks the reluctance to use the painful edge of God's word. This reluctance hides the truth that both pastor and flock are sinners on pilgrimage to holiness. To ignore sin's partial presence is to encourage its power to corrupt the whole.

St. Gregory the Great is not reluctant to use the word's painful edge. He wryly observes, "Look about you and see how full the world is of priests, yet in God's harvest a laborer is rarely to be found. . . . Pray for us that we may have the strength to work on your behalf, that our tongue may not grow weary of exhortation, and that after we have accepted the office of preaching, our silence may not condemn us before the just judge" (St. Gregory the Great, pope).[198]

To accept wholeheartedly the word of God demands that we accept both of its edges!

QUESTION FOR YOUR REFLECTION

What is the difference between the pursuit of peace and the pursuit of appeasement?

Twenty-eighth Week in Ordinary Time

SUNDAY

WORD

"Go up into the hill country; bring timber, and build the house that I may take pleasure in it and receive my glory, says the LORD" (Hag 1:8).

163

REFLECTION

"What are you looking for?" (John 1:38). When Jesus asks this question he opens the door to human life's meaning for all who sincerely search. Two such seekers reply, "Rabbi, . . . where do you stay?" (John 1:38). In his reply Jesus calls them from curiosity to commitment: " 'Come and see,' he answered. So they went to see where he was lodged, and stayed with him that day" (John 1:39).

This gospel narrative disappoints curiosity seekers; it does not disappoint disciples who seek to stay with Jesus in the "house" built with humanity's "timber." This is the house in which "the Word became flesh and made his dwelling among us" (John 1:14).

Jesus' reply, "come and see," invites us "into the hill country" of Christ's incarnation. In the humanity of Mary's womb the Son of God builds the "house" in which God takes pleasure and receives glory. This dwelling place is the marvelous exchange of Christ's divinity and our humanity. Whether we realize it or not, this is "what [we] are . . . looking for."

QUESTION FOR YOUR REFLECTION

In the temple the boy Jesus asks his parents, "Did you not know I had to be in my Father's house?" (Luke 2:49). What meaning does Jesus attach to that question now?

MONDAY

WORD

> *"I will set you as a signet ring; for I have chosen you, says the LORD of hosts"* (Hag 2:23).

REFLECTION

Documents sealed with a king's "signet ring" once carried the full weight of his authority. In the course of time, those chosen to be servants of God likewise became signets of God's presence. Such servants continue to re-member God's presence and make it felt by the authority of "grace, mercy, and peace" (1 Tim 1:2).

Jesus is the signet ring of God's presence. On Mount Tabor, he receives the seal of his Father's imprint as he hears him say, "This is my Son, my Chosen One. Listen to him" (Luke 9:35). The Father of Jesus confirms his ancient promise made to Haggai the prophet: "I will set you as a signet ring; for I have chosen you, says the LORD."

In the sacrament of baptism God chooses us to be "signet ring[s]" of his kingly service. The sacrament of confirmation commits us to the daily service that witnesses Christ's view of kingly authority: "The Son of Man has not come to be served but to serve—to give his life in ransom for the many" (Mark 10:45).

The daily sacrifice of service is evidence that servants of Christ carry the imprint of Christ, God's "signet ring."

QUESTION FOR YOUR REFLECTION

What qualifies you to be a "signet ring" of Christ's kingly presence?

TUESDAY

WORD

"May I ever see you only. . . . May I gaze with love on you alone" (St. Columban, abbot).[199]

REFLECTION

When the scribe asks Jesus, "Which is the first of all the commandments?" (Mark 12:28), Jesus answers without a hint of legality's language: "This is the first: Hear, O Israel! The Lord our God is Lord alone" (Mark 12:29). Jesus' reply suggests that God's lordship is the natural law of love that justifies humankind's reason to exist. It also justifies the reason for all just laws.

Laws are just if they pursue the freedom to achieve wholeness. The priority that Jesus assigns to God's undivided sovereignty moves him to assert: "Therefore you shall love the Lord your God with all your heart, with all your soul, with all your mind, and with all your strength" (Mark 12:30). Wholeness of love is human nature's law because God created all men and women in the likeness of God's image of love (see 1 John 4:16).

Christ translates his first commandment into love for others. He commands that we love our neighbor as we love ourselves. If God is our first law, self-love will commit us to a life of service for others. Truly, "there is no other commandment greater than these" (Mark 12:31).

QUESTION FOR YOUR REFLECTION

In the light of Christ's reply to the scribe, what is the natural law for everyone?

WEDNESDAY

WORD

"The lamp set upon the lampstand is Jesus Christ. . . .
He has designated holy Church the lampstand" (St. Maximus the Confessor, abbot).[200]

REFLECTION

The Church's mission is to serve as the "lampstand" for the light of Christ. This is its glory because fidelity to service allows the rays of God's word to illuminate the minds of all men and women. The Church knows that fidelity to God's word of service remains unshakable in the face of persecution that permits the light of Christ to shine more brightly.

This persecution never abates and, indeed, is evidence that the Church's service to Christ the light of the world is effective. For example, the Church today confronts the darkness of attitudes that strike at the roots of human life. It refuses to succumb to the sham of an alleged sacredness that blesses privacy of choice with sovereignty over life itself.

The darkness that leaves human destiny to human discretion blinds pro-choice proponents to the choice of which God speaks: "I have set before you life and death, the blessing and the curse. Choose life, then, that you and your descendants may live, by loving the LORD, your God, heeding his voice, and holding fast to him. For that will mean life for

166

you, a long life for you to live on the land which the LORD swore he would give to your fathers Abraham, Isaac and Jacob" (Deut 30:19-20).

QUESTION FOR YOUR REFLECTION

Choice is a blessing. When does it become a curse?

THURSDAY

WORD

> *"It is not enough that you are moved by the will, for you are drawn also by desire"* (St. Augustine, bishop).[201]

REFLECTION

We are happy when there is a consistency between what we will and what we desire. When the latter is inconsistent with the former, there is not only unhappiness but also the absence of freedom. Every human being wants to be happy but, alas, desires ways to happiness that reap the bondage to addiction. "Addiction and freedom" is a contradiction in terms.

What one really longs for is an imperishable destiny. Such a longing can never be expelled but can be silenced by the lie that wraps this world's perishables in the mantle of transcendence. "I am happy because I *have* everything I desire" is a lie. To desire only what one can *possess* of this world's perishables is to live divorced from the longing to *be* in the likeness of God's beauty, goodness, and truth.

For St. Augustine, desire is not an evil. It is a spouse of the will that hungers for "wisdom, justice, truth [and] eternal life."[202] When these imperishables are desired, we are happy and free. "Show me one who is full of longing, one who is hungry, one who is a pilgrim and suffering from thirst in the desert of this world, eager for the fountain in the homeland of eternity; show me someone like that, and he knows what I mean."[203]

QUESTION FOR YOUR REFLECTION

The taking of unborn human life under the pretext of freedom of choice is a contradiction. Why?

WORD

"I have no pleasure in you, says the LORD *of hosts; neither will I accept any sacrifice from your hands"* (Mal 1:10).

REFLECTION

God takes "no pleasure" in those who offer sacrifice touched by their hands but untouched by hearts made for eternal life. Such sacrifice is hypocrisy.

Sacrifice slaughters the spirit when it exalts only the self. St. Augustine writes of the spirit that takes sacrifice to heart before it touches the hands. "Every work that [unites us] with God in a holy [communion] is a true sacrifice" (St. Augustine, bishop).[204]

St. Augustine links his view of "true sacrifice" to St. Paul's exhortation to the Romans: "I beg you through the mercy of God to offer your bodies as a living sacrifice holy and acceptable to God, your spiritual worship. Do not conform yourselves to this age but be transformed by the renewal of your mind, so that you may judge what is God's will, what is good, pleasing and perfect" (Rom 12:1-2).

QUESTION FOR YOUR REFLECTION

What is the sacrifice that the Eucharist pleads for us to unite with Christ's?

WORD

"In his spirit we have been brought to life and gathered into unity" (Pastoral Constitution on the Church ln the Modern World).[205]

REFLECTION

The image of human existence is God's communion of three persons. This communion is life itself, the life of which Jesus speaks: "Just as the Father possesses life in himself, so has he granted it to the Son to have life in himself. . . . I came that they might have life and have it to the full" (John 5:26; 10:10). This is why Jesus sent "his spirit [that we might be] brought to life and gathered into unity."

We are alive not because we breathe; we are alive because the breath of God's Spirit-presence bonds us into a communion that sets humanity apart from all other creatures. God's Spirit unites us into a communion that is *like* God's. This communion justifies our earthly existence but even more importantly, justifies us to live in communion with God forever.

At its Eucharistic celebrations the Church prays:

> All life, all holiness comes from you through your Son, Jesus Christ our Lord, by the working of the Holy Spirit. From age to age you gather a people to yourself, so that from east to west a perfect offering may be made to the glory of your name (Eucharistic Prayer III).[206]

QUESTION FOR YOUR REFLECTION

What is the connection between "life" and "unity"?

Twenty-ninth Week in Ordinary Time

SUNDAY

WORD

> "Why . . . should [God] ask us to pray when he knows what we need before we ask him" (St. Augustine, bishop).[207]

REFLECTION

Unceasing prayer opens us to the will of God dwelling within us. This discovery arouses desire for union with God, a union that moves Jesus to say, "Blest are they who hunger and thirst for holiness; they shall have their fill" (Matt 5:6).

Martha's petitions for help with "all the details of hospitality" (Luke 10:40) leads her to the discovery that "one thing only is required. Mary has chosen the better portion and she shall not be deprived of it" (Luke 10:42). That "one thing" is the hunger and thirst for a heart wholly hospitable to Christ. When prayer is unceasing, hearts are so enlarged that "the details of hospitality" no longer seem important.

Does God know what we desire? Of course! But do *we* know what we *really* want? We don't, because although "[God's] gift is very great, our capacity is too small to receive it. That is why we are told, "Enlarge your desires, do not bear the yoke with unbelievers."[208]

Prayer is not information passed on to God; prayer is the transformation of hearts enlarged to make room for God. That's the "better portion" of which we "shall not be deprived."

QUESTION FOR YOUR REFLECTION

Those who no longer hunger for food die of starvation. What are the prospects for those who cease praying?

MONDAY

WORD

"Let us always desire the happy life from the Lord God and always pray for it; . . . otherwise, the desire that began to grow lukewarm may grow [cold] altogether and may be totally extinguished unless it is repeatedly stirred into flame" (St. Augustine, bishop).[209]

REFLECTION

A great Polish pianist, Jan Paderewski, once commented: "If I would neglect to practice one day, I would notice it. If I would fail to practice a week, the music critics would surely notice it. If I would fail to practice a month, you, my public, would notice it."

As with masters of the piano, so with masters of prayer. Their daily practice brings forth a perfection that cannot be hidden. Their lives sing the "new song" (Ps 96:1) of God's presence, a presence that moves them to exclaim, "The favors of the LORD I will sing forever;/ through all generations my mouth shall proclaim your faithfulness" (Ps 89:2).

We pray not to get God's attention; we pray that God might get ours. Prayer is not what we do to God; prayer is what God does for us. Prayer does not move God; prayer enables us to move toward the living presence of God within us. In awe we join St. Paul, who writes, "Eye has not seen, ear has not heard,/ nor has it so much as dawned on man what God has prepared for those who love him" (1 Cor 2:9).

QUESTION FOR YOUR REFLECTION

"If my prayers are not answered, why should I pray?" How would you respond to this?

TUESDAY

WORD

> *"Any man or woman who goes to the king in the inner court without being summoned, suffers . . . death, unless the king extends to him the golden scepter"* (Esth 4:11).

REFLECTION

The Jewish people had been condemned to death. Their spokesman, Mordecai, pleads with Queen Esther, once in his care, to intercede in behalf of her own people. She rationalizes that, except for the king's offer of the "golden scepter," death is her penalty if she appears uninvited before him.

Mordecai's reply is prophetic: "Do not imagine that because you are in the king's palace, you alone of all the Jews will escape. Even if you now remain silent, relief and deliverance will come to the Jews from another source. . . . Who knows but that it was for a time like this that you obtained the royal dignity" (Esth 4:13-14). It is from this kindly but firm reply that the Jewish Queen Esther understands that she has already been offered the "golden scepter" of God's will.

St. Augustine writes, "When we say: 'Your will be done on earth as it is in heaven,' we are asking [God] to make us obedient so that his will might be done in us as it is done in heaven" (St. Augustine, bishop).[210]

Prayer that rationalizes wearies God, who already extends to us the "golden scepter" of Jesus Christ, empowering us to be instruments of "grace, mercy, and peace" (2 Tim 1:2). We pray that we might accept God's "golden scepter" so that *in us* God's will might be done on earth as it is in heaven.

QUESTION FOR YOUR REFLECTION

God's will is already done. Why does Jesus ask us to pray, "Your will be done" (Matt 6:10)?

WEDNESDAY

WORD

"If you study every word of the petitions of scripture, you will find, I think, nothing that is not included in the Lord's prayer" (St. Augustine, bishop).[211]

REFLECTION

One of St. Pius X's last pontifical acts was his refusal to bless troops of war. When the Austrian ambassador asked for this blessing, the pontiff angrily replied, "I bless peace, not war!"[212]

St. Pius X refused a petition inconsistent with the mind of Christ. And so it is with prayerful petitions. Their integrity is tested by the Lord's Prayer. If our petitions are consistent with that prayer, they find room in the heart of Christ. His heart is closed to prayers infected with attitudes of selfishness, anger, bitterness, and revenge. But it is open to prayer that radiates thoughts of peace.

The only language God understands is love. Hearts, not tongues, speak this language. When we speak from hearts with room only for peace, we find God listening. Such hearts move Jesus to repeat, "Ask, and you will receive. Seek, and you will find. Knock, and it will be opened to you" (Matt 7:7).

QUESTION FOR YOUR REFLECTION

Prayer in Christ will always be heard. What does "in Christ" mean?

WORD

"[If God] does not take [affliction] away, we must not imagine that we are being forgotten by him but, because of our loving endurance of evil, must await greater blessings in its place" (St. Augustine, bishop).[213]

REFLECTION

Those whose prayer knocks at the door of worldly strengths are knocking at the wrong door. The aim of prayer is not to pass over from worldly poverty to worldly abundance. Prayer aims to pass through the door with which Jesus identifies himself: "I am the gate. Whoever enters through me will be safe" (John 10:9).

This "gate" leads to a life of joy and peace completely foreign to this world's strengths. Strange as it seems, affliction is the passport required for passage into the life that Jesus came for us to live. "Therefore," St. Paul asserts, "I am content with weakness, with mistreatment, with distress, with persecutions and difficulties for the sake of Christ; for when I am powerless, it is then that I am strong" (2 Cor 12:10).

The "poor in spirit" are "blest" (Matt 5:3) because they discover in their afflictions what Jesus means when he says, "I came that they might have life and have it to the full (John 10:10). As they experience the warmth of God's intimacy enveloping them, they rejoice that what they have become in prayer is far more enriching than that which, happily, prayer leaves unanswered.

QUESTION FOR YOUR REFLECTION

What is God saying to you in his silence to your unanswered prayers?

WORD

"The Spirit moves the saints to plead with sighs too deep for words by inspiring in them a desire for the great and as yet unknown reality that we look forward to with patience" (St. Augustine, bishop).[214]

REFLECTION

St. Augustine echoes St. Paul's, "We do not know how to pray as we ought; but the Spirit . . . makes intercession for us with groanings that cannot be expressed in speech" (Rom 8:26). What are these "groanings," and how can they be detected within us?

They are God's longings for every person's communion with God, with the saints, and with one another. These longings are "too deep" for human expression. Like breathing, God's longings are the unceasing sighs of the Holy Spirit's "groanings" for us to share a life incomparable to this world's version.

God's longings can be detected in our desire to be with God especially in times of affliction. Jesus sees such desire in the dying thief who groans, "Jesus, remember me when you enter upon your reign" (Luke 23:42). This dying man's sighs enable a spark of the Holy Spirit's "groanings" to ignite twenty centuries of hope in men and women who fill up "what is lacking in the sufferings of Christ" (Col 1:24).

The one prayer that God answers is that we long to be with God on earth and in heaven. This communion is the will of God and is the reason we pray as Jesus desires: "Your kingdom come, your will be done on earth as it is in heaven" (Matt 6:10). God longs for our company with sighs that cannot be expressed in speech."

QUESTION FOR YOUR REFLECTION

Why did Jesus link "your kingdom come" with "your will be done"?

WORD

> *"Turn, O Jacob, and receive her: walk by her light to-*
> *ward splendor"* (Bar 4:2).

REFLECTION

The sixth decade of this century marked the emergence of the "me generation," who marched to the tune of Frank Sinatra's declaration for a life lived "my way." This song's lyrics suggest the contradiction of a doing-your-thing attitude in a nation pledging "one nation, under God, indivisible, with liberty and justice for all."

The "my way" attitude has nourished an attitude that upholds choices in which the sovereignty of "me" endangers "liberty and justice for all." Those who opt for living life "my way" live lives bereft of the priceless gift of wisdom.

Wisdom sheds light that illumines choice of communion with God and humankind over the folly of the individualism that has no problem with excising human life. Baruch's prayer in behalf of wisdom is as timely today as it was long before the birth of Christ. "Turn, O Jacob, and receive her: walk by her light toward splendor."

QUESTION FOR YOUR REFLECTION

Why are choices limited only to earthly aspirations evidence of wisdom's absence?

Thirtieth Week in Ordinary Time

SUNDAY

WORD

> *"Let us consider the care with which [God] provides the*
> *whole of creation"* (St. Clement, pope).[215]

REFLECTION

Even to wonder "Do I have Alzheimer's disease?" is evidence that one doesn't. Similarly, even to wonder "Am I in the state of mortal sin?" is evidence that perhaps one isn't. The very question suggests the care that has not been deadened by one's preoccupation with living life "my way." Care for human life is evidence that one's "sense of sin" is not dead.

People who care about the state of their relationship with God sense the harmony and balance that link all men and women to their *immortal* destiny. This sensitivity reveals the presence of the wisdom that lights up the lives of caring people. This wisdom links men and women with God's infinite care for human life.

"Let us fix our gaze on the Father and Creator of the whole world," St. Clement writes, "and let us hold on to his peace and blessings, his splendid and surpassing gifts. Let us contemplate him in our thoughts and with our mind's eye reflect upon the peaceful and restrained unfolding of his plan; let us consider the care with which he provides for the whole of creation."[216]

QUESTION FOR YOUR REFLECTION

Human life has been created for a purpose that links it to an immortal destiny. What change of purpose reduces human destiny to mortal dimensions?

MONDAY

WORD

"God formed man to be imperishable; the image of his own nature he made him" (Wis 2:23).

REFLECTION

Governments rationalize when they term stockpiles of weapons "peacemakers." The Book of Wisdom refers to such rationalizing:

Let our strength be our norm of justice;
  for weakness proves itself useless. . . .
Let us see whether his words be true;
  let us find out what will happen to him (Wis 2:11, 17).

The "norm of justice" is not "our strength." God refuses tests of divine strength that invite magic rather than revelation. Such is the devil's test when, in the desert, he urges Jesus to throw himself down from the temple heights under the pretext that God "will bid his angels watch over" him (Luke 4:9). Jesus replies: "You shall not put the Lord your God to the test" (Luke 4:12).

The "norm of justice" is humility. The humble possess a wisdom that lets them see themselves as God sees them. God sees all men and women as the inheritors of imperishability, a destiny that justifies human existence. This destiny is hidden from the stockpilers of weaponry, who regard humility as the "weakness [that] proves itself useless." They reject the strength of humility, which inherits an eternity of imperishability.

The wise rejoice as they take to heart Jesus' invitation to embrace his strength: "Come to me, all you who are weary and find life burdensome, and I will refresh you. Take my yoke upon your shoulders and learn from me, for I am gentle and humble of heart. Your souls will find rest, for my yoke is easy and my burden light" (Matt 11:28-30).

QUESTION FOR YOUR REFLECTION

Why is humility a strength?

TUESDAY

WORD

"Nothing is impossible for God except to tell a lie" (St. Clement, pope).[217]

REFLECTION

The souls of the just are in the hand of God,
  and no torment shall touch them (Wis 3:1).

The diabolical mind first encounters humanity in the garden of Eden. The substance of that encounter is the lie whose promises eventually end in torment for all who subscribe to the serpent's description of human purpose: "You certainly will not die! No, God knows well that the moment you eat of it you will be like gods who know what is good and what is bad" (Gen 3:4-5).

This lie has become the matrix of all sins. Couched only within the parameters of sense experience, it proposes to hand over to human creaturehood the crown of God's sovereignty. Succumbing to that lie, Adam and Eve trade God's lordship for a creaturehood destined for perishability. It is the betrayal of betrayals.

"The souls of the just are in the hand of God." Who are the just? They are all who believe that, in Christ, humankind has been reowned by God. The just believe that in Christ's resurrection, God exposes the colossal lie that assigns lordship to the fruits of this world. The just believe that on the tree of his cross Jesus destroys the lie about Eden's tree and enables God to raise up humanity by a strength foreign to this world.

For all who believe this truth, "no torment shall touch them."

QUESTION FOR YOUR REFLECTION

How is freedom of private choice a repetition of the lie, "You will be like gods who know what is good and what is bad"?

WEDNESDAY

WORD

*"Hearken, you who are in power over the multitude
and lord it over throngs of peoples!
Because authority was given you by the LORD
and sovereignty by the Most High,
who shall probe your works and scrutinize your
counsels!"* (Wis 6:2-3).

REFLECTION

Human dignity is at the heart of civil authority's reason to rule. Civil authority is wise when it understands wisdom's reason for human dignity. Wisdom directs authority to a service based on a law that is natural to all. This natural law requires that all men and women live in an atmosphere where their imperative to share the image and likeness of God can be realized.

Authority veers away from wisdom when it focuses on vested interests. When authority's perception of its worth is located in these interests, subservience *to them* becomes the expectation vested interests have of both rulers and the ruled. Such expectation leads to injustice and its violation of human dignity.

Authority is genuine when it serves the natural law that requires concern for all. This concern is the interest vested in the heart of Christ and in the hearts of people united to him. It is the interest that survives all others because it is from God, "who shall probe [authority's] works and scrutinize [its] counsels!"

QUESTION FOR YOUR REFLECTION

In the mind of genuine authority, where is the primary source of its rule?

THURSDAY

WORD

> *"Such things as are hidden I learned and such as are*
> *plain;*
> *for Wisdom, the artificer of all, taught me"* (Wis 7:21-22).

REFLECTION

Mystery is not unexplainability. It is hiddenness in search of revelation. Like life hidden in a seed, it awaits liberation so that it might be visibly united with Wisdom, who longs to unveil the inexhaustible presence of God. Wisdom's light is ready to radiate the undisclosed dimensions of beauty, goodness, and truth in creatures destined to be their reflections.

God is mystery whose hiddenness longs to be disclosed from the mystery of each person's uniqueness. "An impress of Wisdom," writes St. Athanasius, "has been created in us and in all his works. Therefore, the true Wisdom which shaped the world claims for himself all that bears his image" (St. Athanasius, bishop).[218]

The wise are not necessarily the knowledgeable. They are those who stand humbly before God as doors open for his hiddenness to be revealed. It is the wise who dare say, "Such things as are hidden I learned and such as are plain; for Wisdom, the artificer of all, taught me."

QUESTION FOR YOUR REFLECTION

Besides revealing that which has been hidden, what is Wisdom's role for "such [things] as are plain"?

FRIDAY

WORD

"The word of God is plainly shown in all its strength and wisdom to those who seek out Christ, who is the word, the power and the wisdom of God" (Baldwin of Canterbury, bishop).[219]

REFLECTION

Wisdom is more than an attribute of God. It is "the Word became flesh" (John 1:14) so that all men and women might share and disclose "the word, the power and the wisdom of God." Wisdom is humanity's espousal to Christ, from which nuptial there is born the wisdom that "reaches from end to end mightily and governs all things well" (Wis 8:1).

The search for wisdom leads to mystery's door. Those who fail to enter that door under the pretext of mystery's alleged unexplainability likewise fail to find wisdom. When believers are content with unexplainability they risk the exchange of faith for the fatalism that blinds them to the life of God's Word.

"This word of God is living," writes Bishop Baldwin of Canterbury. "The Father gave it life in itself, just as he has life in himself. For this reason it is life, as [Christ] says of himself, 'I am the way, the truth, and the life.' Since he is life, he is both living and life-giving."[220]

There is life when there is search. To search for Christ is to find Christ. This is the search that gives birth to wisdom waiting to be born from the hiddenness of human life graced to be the spouse of Christ. "If any of you is without wisdom," writes St. James, "let him ask it from the God who gives generously and ungrudgingly to all, and it will be given him" (Jas 1:5).

QUESTION FOR YOUR REFLECTION

Someone has written that those content to live with the shades drawn never see the light of the sun. How does this apply to the search for wisdom?

SATURDAY

WORD

> *"Indeed, before you the whole universe is as a grain from*
> *a balance,*
> *or a drop of morning dew come down upon the earth"*
(Wis 11:22).

REFLECTION

Alas, hardly noticed at each Eucharist are the words that accompany the mingling of a few drops of water with wine: "By the mystery of this water and wine may we come to share in the divinity of Christ, who humbled himself to share in our humanity" (Liturgy of the Eucharist).[221] Imagine! We who measure but "a grain" of wheat or "a drop of morning dew come down upon the earth" now "share in the divinity of Christ" because Christ "humbled himself to share in our humanity."

"I remind you," writes St. Paul to Timothy, "to stir into flame the gift of God bestowed . . . on you" (2 Tim 1:6). These words apply to the gift of Christ's divinity in communion with our humanity. In this marvelous exchange Jesus bonds us with his Father, the Holy Spirit and the communion of saints. The awareness of this gift is "stir[red] into flame" whenever we celebrate the Eucharist—the good gift—which Christ longs for us to "do . . . as a remembrance of me" (Luke 22:19).

St. Catherine of Siena records God the Father saying to her: "I gave [humankind] a memory to recall my goodness, for I have wanted [all] to share in my own power. . . . In my loving care I did all this, so that [all] could know me and perceive my goodness and rejoice to see me for ever."[222]

QUESTION FOR YOUR REFLECTION

What would Christ mean if he asked you, "What are you worth?"

Thirty-first Week in Ordinary Time

SUNDAY

WORD

"Peace is . . . the fruit also of love; love goes beyond what justice can conceive" (Pastoral Constitution on the Church in the Modern World).[223]

REFLECTION

Justice bears the fruit of peace but love is the root of justice. The story of the widow and her mite reveals this distinction. Noticing the widow who drops two copper coins into the treasury, Jesus comments to his disciples: "I assure you, this poor widow has put in more than all the rest. They make contributions out if their surplus, but she from her want has given what she could not afford—every penny she had to live on" (Luke 21:3-4).

The widow relates to God not by what she possesses but by who she is. She is a child of God whose poverty allows the roots of her life to sink into the soil of God's love. This soil reveals her dignity and the justice that bears the fruit of peace. She gives "from her want" of this world's treasures, and from that love she "has put in more than all the rest."

When hatred replaces love the injustice of war destroys peace. This hatred takes root in those for whom God is worth no more than "contributions out of their surplus." There is no room in hearts that want both "God and money" (Matt 6:24). When there is room only for the welcome of God, there will always be peace.

QUESTION FOR YOUR REFLECTION

How would you answer this question: "But didn't the Pharisees give more than the widow?"

MONDAY

WORD

"To build peace, the causes of human discord must be eliminated, . . . especially the violations of justice" (Pastoral Constitution on the Church in the Modern World).[224]

REFLECTION

The first book of Maccabees opens with an account of Jewish apostasy in the face of open persecution. Side by side with apostasy, however, there also runs the account of Jewish loyalty from a statesmanlike family whose civil disobedience to tyranny reveals an inner obedience to their loyalty to God. It was this inner obedience that saved God's people from extinction.

There is another side of apostasy's coin. Often there appears an outer dedication that masks the apostasy of inner disloyalty. This facade covers hardened attitudes fomenting divisions that prevent peace. Unless there is consistency between outward displays of loyalty and inner attitudes of faithfulness, peace will be but a dream.

The Fathers of the Second Vatican Council write: "We must all undergo a change of heart. . . . Unless antagonism and hatred are abandoned, unless binding and honest agreements are concluded, [humankind], already in grave peril, may well face in spite of its marvelous advance in knowledge that day of disaster when it knows no other peace than the awful peace of death."[225]

The apostasy we can see is not as destructive of peace as the one that lies hidden.

QUESTION FOR YOUR REFLECTION

Where is the apostasy that keeps racism alive in America?

TUESDAY

WORD

"In order to foster and encourage cooperation among men [and women], the Church must be present in the community of nations" (Pastoral Constitution on the Church in the Modern World).[226]

REFLECTION

When a sponge is placed in water, it draws the water to itself. When a bit of yeast is placed in a measure of flour, it yields its identity to the flour it serves.

Sponges allow themselves to be infiltrated; yeast leavens. Jesus came as leaven for the whole world. "To what shall I compare the reign of God? It is like yeast which a woman took to knead into three measures of flour until the whole mass of dough began to rise" (Luke 13:21). It was to his Church that Jesus yielded his leavening mission of raising the whole world to share the peace of his kingdom.

Before the Church asks obedience from others, she first obeys her mission of service to society's poor and unwanted. She reiterates Christ's assurance, "The Son of Man has not come to be served but to serve—to give his life in ransom for the many" (Mark 10:45).

Christ's action in the Church leavens society so that the communion of justice and peace, rooted in love, might be more than a dream.

When the Church is present in a community of nations to serve rather than be served, there will be peace.

QUESTION FOR YOUR REFLECTION

Communism infiltrates; Christianity leavens. What is the difference?

WORD

"Victory in war does not depend upon the size of the army, but on strength that comes from Heaven" (1 Macc 3:19).

REFLECTION

The psalmist describes God's mirth at kings and princes plotting war:

The kings of the earth rise up,
    and the princes conspire together
    against the LORD and against his anointed:
"Let us break their fetters
    and cast their bonds from us!"
He who is throned in heaven laughs;
    the LORD derides them. . . .
    Happy are all who take refuge in him! (Ps 2:2-4, 11).

Faith is weakest when nations call weapons "peacemakers." Faith is strongest when its peacemakers are justice and mercy. "It is of this kind of faith," writes St. Cyril of Jerusalem, "that it is said: 'If you have faith like a grain of mustard seed.' "[227] "Justice and peace shall kiss" (Ps 85:11) when but a "grain" of faith is the weapon of "all who take refuge in him."

With but a "mustard seed" of faith a thief implores Jesus, his crucified companion, "Remember me when you enter upon your reign" (Luke 23:42). Jesus breaks the "fetters" and the "bonds" of this man's life of crime when he replies, "I assure you: this day you will be with me in paradise" (Luke 23:43). When these two companions in death enter paradise, "justice and peace" embrace.

QUESTION FOR YOUR REFLECTION

Peace is the "strength that comes from Heaven." What is the way to that strength?

WORD

"In learning and professing the faith, you must accept and retain only the Church's present tradition, confirmed as it is by the scriptures" (St. Cyril of Jerusalem, bishop).[228]

REFLECTION

Tradition is not confined to the past. It also nourishes both the present and the future. It asks the present for the care that reverently receives it; it asks both past and present for the care that creatively hands it on.

Orthodoxy is care shown for the rightness of truth received and handed on. It cares for the substance of truth ever ancient and ever new. It scrupulously attends to the substance of the Church's creeds so that new hearts might be nourished. "I order you," writes St. Cyril of Jerusalem, "to retain this creed for your nourishment throughout life and never to accept any alternative."[229]

New hearts are not "alternatives" to tradition. They are like new days open to receive the ever ancient light and warmth of the sun. Those who open themselves *today* to the light and warmth of the Church's ancient creed nourish faith even the size of a "mustard seed." St. Cyril comments, "Just as the mustard seed contains in a small grain many branches, so [the creed's] brief statement of faith keeps in its heart . . . all the religious truth . . . found in Old and New Testament alike."[230]

QUESTION FOR YOUR REFLECTION

What is the difference between substance of faith and customs of faith? Which of the two relates to tradition?

186

WORD

"For if he were not expecting the fallen to rise again, it would have been useless and foolish to pray for them in death" (2 Macc 12:44).

REFLECTION

Prayer for the dead acknowledges the permanency of life. We pray for the dead because we do not accept death's visible evidence of final separation. Faith in Christ's word, "I came that they might have life" (John 10:10), strengthens us to pray, "Lord, for your faithful people, life is changed, not ended" (Preface of Christian Death I).[231]

St. Gregory Nazianzen speaks of life in Christ: " 'What is man that you are mindful of him?' What is this new mystery surrounding me? I am both small and great, both lowly and exalted, mortal and immortal, earthly and heavenly. I am to be buried with Christ and to rise again with him, to become coheir with him, a son of God, and indeed God himself."[232]

Prayer for the dead nourishes, enlivens, and strengthens faith in our communion with Christ and the communion of saints. This communion moves us to pray, "life is changed, not ended." Faith in communion with life in Christ and all who have shared death with him moves us to exclaim, "Precious in the eyes of the LORD is the death of his faithful ones" (Ps 116:15).

QUESTION FOR YOUR REFLECTION

Bishops and priests formerly vested in black at masses for the dead. Why do white vestments now state a more accurate meaning of death?

SATURDAY

WORD

"Death must be active within us if life also is to be active within us. 'Life' is life after death, a life that is a blessing" (St. Ambrose, bishop).[233]

REFLECTION

The life of heroic Judas Maccabeus ends on a dismal note: "Then Judas fell, and the rest fled" (1 Macc 9:18). These words recall the dismal lyrics of the song that asks, "Is that all there is?"

In a certain sense death is final. It ends conflict with the perishability that characterizes earthly life's tenure. But equally real is the birth that springs from death. Death gives birth to life's fullness when the demands of earthly existence no longer impede its blessing.

At the Eucharist we proclaim death's liberation of life as we pray, "When we eat this bread and drink this cup, we proclaim your death, Lord Jesus, until you come in glory" (Memorial Acclamation C).[234] Christ's death continuously opens the door of human life's rebirth and its call to follow in the steps of Christ's passover from death to resurrection.

Willingly accepting our passover pilgrimage, Jesus confidently confronts the near desperate plea "Is that all there is?"

> I solemnly assure you,
> unless the grain of wheat falls to the earth and dies,
> it remains just a grain of wheat.
> But if it dies,
> it produces much fruit (John 12:24).

QUESTION FOR YOUR REFLECTION

What blessings have come from sacrifices asked of you?

Thirty-second Week in Ordinary Time

SUNDAY

WORD

> "Daniel was resolved not to defile himself with the king's food or wine" (Dan 1:8).

REFLECTION

Acts of self-denial are not credentials for procuring God's favor. These exercises are credentials for seeing the blessings we already enjoy *in Christ.*

Daniel the prophet honors his resolve "not to defile himself with the king's food or wine" and in so doing gives evidence of a wisdom that astounds the king. Daniel lives the life of "a resident alien" (see Ezek 47:23) from whose interior regions of faithfulness emerges a wisdom foreign to all who are ignorant of God's presence.

Daniel and his companions' esteem for God goes beyond kingly cuisine. Their lives of self-denial reveal blessings obvious to all. "In any question of wisdom or prudence which the king put to them, he found them ten times better than all the magicians and enchanters in his kingdom" (Dan 1:20).

Saints are people whose esteem for Jesus Christ fully occupies their hearts. This esteem is the fruit of a discipline that frees them from the blindness that holds high esteem only for this world's treasures. Shunning them by acts of self-denial, they find within themselves a pearl of great price, Jesus Christ. His way of sacrifice is their credential for sainthood.

QUESTION FOR YOUR REFLECTION

We lose faith when we are blind to the presence of God. How is this blindness healed?

MONDAY

WORD

*"To you in your bed there came thoughts about . . .
the future. . . . To me also this mystery has been revealed"*
(Dan 2:29-30).

REFLECTION

Well-built walls never collapse if they are built on rock. "Anyone who hears my words," Jesus exhorts, "and puts them into practice is like the wise man who built his house on rock" (Matt 7:24). Jesus speaks with authority because he built his whole life on the foundation stone of his Father.

When the commandments are the "rock" of our lives, that may be evidence that we confuse walls with foundations. The foundation of all commandments is the law that prefaces them: "I, the LORD, am your God, who brought you out of the land of Egypt, that place of slavery. You shall not have other gods besides me" (Exod 20:2-3).

When a scribe asks Jesus, "Which is the first of all the commandments?" (Mark 12:28). Jesus echoes his Father's preface to commandments: "Hear, O Israel! The Lord our God is Lord alone!" (Mark 12:29). For Jesus, "this is the first" (Mark 12:29), yes, the "rock," upon which the wise build the household of their faith.

Dreams of the future prefaced with "the Lord our God is Lord alone" are built on solid rock. With this as the foundation, dreams are really mystery awaiting revelation in "anyone who hears my words and puts them into practice."

QUESTION FOR YOUR REFLECTION

Why is acknowledgment of Jesus Christ the foundation of all commandments?

TUESDAY

WORD

"I see four men unfettered and unhurt, walking in the fire, and the fourth looks like a son of God" (Dan 3:92).

REFLECTION

Because repentance often carries a punitive ring tolled by bell ringers of doom, it fails to ring glad tidings of the renewal that rings its true meaning.

Repentance is the renewal of which Ezekiel speaks: "Cast away from you all the crimes you have committed, and make for yourselves a new heart and a new spirit. . . . I have no pleasure in the death of anyone who dies, says the Lord GOD. Return and live!" (Ezek 18:31-32). The sign of repentance is the joy of "a new heart and a new spirit" in those who have returned to companionship with God.

Repentance renews both body and spirit. "Nor must any of you say," writes a second-century homilist, "that our bodies will not share in the judgment, nor rise again. . . . Our bodies are the temple of God, and as such we must guard them, for even as we were called in the body, so shall we also be judged in the body."[235]

Life on earth is a journey of renewal begun in baptism. From waters that touch our bodies there begins the awakening to the world of God's presence within and around us. This awakening to God's kingdom is repentance. It presents us to God "unfettered and unhurt" in companionship with the Son of God.

QUESTION FOR YOUR REFLECTION

How is Christ's human presence denied when Christians reserve renewal only to the soul?

WEDNESDAY

WORD

"TEKEL, you have been weighed on the scales and found wanting" (Dan 5:27).

REFLECTION

Scales report weight. They pass judgment on the claims of weight.

There is also a scale that reports the weight of our relationship with God. This scale is justice. It weighs the equality with which Jesus Christ graced all men and women to realize their glory. In Christ, then, humanity has been placed on the scales of justice and "found [not] wanting."

What is the weight of humanity's dignity on the scales of justice? It is the will of God that there be a graced balance between our humanity and God's divinity. This is the balance of which St. John speaks: "See what love the Father has bestowed on us in letting us be called children of God! . . . We are God's children now; what we shall later be has not yet come to light. We know that when it comes to light we shall be like him" (1 John 3:1-2).

The weight of God is the glory of God radiating from lives that balance what people say they believe with the way they live what they say. When word and deed are balanced, holiness is the evidence that the scales of justice accurately report.

QUESTION FOR YOUR REFLECTION

What is the weight that the scales of justice accurately report?

THURSDAY

WORD

"Why is the Lord's name blasphemed? Because we say one thing and do another" (second-century homily).[236]

REFLECTION

Outwardly Judas Iscariot is a follower of Christ; inwardly he is a betrayer. His kiss of affection turns out to be his decree of execution.

Judas has a face for Christ and a face for money. With the one he kisses Christ; with the other he accepts money as the price for his betrayal. He tries both faces and when he discovers that he can no longer walk in both directions, he realizes the hypocrisy that blasphemes the name of Christ.

"Why is the Lord's name blasphemed? Because we say one thing and do another. When they hear the words of God on our lips, unbelievers are amazed at their beauty and power, but when they see that those words have no effect in our lives, their admiration turns to scorn, and they dismiss such words as myths and fairy tales."[237]

Blasphemy is the sword that severs the link between Spirit and humanity. This marriage is the will of God on earth as it is in the communion of God and saints. When that communion is seen on earth, evangelization is inevitable. "If the Holy Spirit is joined to [the Church], this body can receive an immortal life that is wonderful beyond words, for the blessings God has made ready for his chosen ones surpass all human powers of description."[238]

QUESTION FOR YOUR REFLECTION

Frequently Pope John Paul II speaks of reevangelization. How does that word apply to Christians?

FRIDAY

WORD

"A very good way of atoning for our sins is by being generous to the poor. Fasting is better than prayer, but almsgiving surpasses both, for 'love covers a multitude of sins'" (second-century homily).[239]

REFLECTION

When fasting and almsgiving are absent, prayer is ineffective. Jesus insists, "None of those who cry out, 'Lord, Lord,' will enter the kingdom of God but only the one who does the will of my Father in heaven" (Matt 7:21).

The will of the Father requires that the prayer of lips passes over to the prayer of heart. Fasting and almsgiving open our hearts so that the heart of God's will might enter and speak: "As often as you did it for one of my least brothers, you did it for me" (Matt 25:40). Fasting sets the stage for the sincerity that clearly sees God's compassion; almsgiving is evidence that sincerity has moved prayer to compassion.

Prayer becomes effective when our hearts will what God wills. When there is consistency between words prayed and deeds done, prayer stands before the throne of God in the good company of fasting and almsgiving. This is a "very good way of atoning for our sins," for "by relieving the poor, [we] will be relieved of [our] sins."[240] Prayer for forgiveness is effective when It shares the company of fasting and almsgiving.

QUESTION FOR YOUR REFLECTION

What is the passover that assures the effectiveness of prayer?

SATURDAY

WORD

"Competing as we are in the pursuit of the living God, the training which we receive in this present life will make us worthy to be crowned in the life to come" (second-century homily).[241]

REFLECTION

It is folly to link education only to the young. How comic to think of graduation as the end of schooling! This attitude is disastrous when graduation ends schooling in the ways of God. Because God is infinite, schooling in the ways of God is a lifetime pursuit.

After the prophet Daniel sees a vision of heaven, he confesses to the angel, "I heard, but I did not understand; so I asked, 'My lord, what follows this?' 'Go, Daniel,' he said, 'because the words are to be kept secret and sealed until the end time'" (Dan 12:8-9).

Not in one vision can the secrecy of God's identity be revealed. Gradually God's hiddenness unfolds within us so that we might be strengthened to resist the demands of our unrepentant selves.

St. Peter pleads, "Stay sober and alert. Your opponent the devil is prowling like a roaring lion looking for someone to devour. Resist him, solid in your faith, realizing that the brotherhood of believers is undergoing the same sufferings throughout the world" (1 Pet 5:8-9).

This resistance is a lifetime schooling whose graduation is Christ's resurrection giving us tenure in an eternity of joy.

QUESTION FOR YOUR REFLECTION

Why must schooling in the ways of God be continuous?

Thirty-third Week in Ordinary Time

WORD

"Fear not, O Land!
exult and rejoice!
for the LORD has done great things" (Joel 2:21).

REFLECTION

God lives by law rooted in the nature of God. "God is love" (1 John 4:8) is God's law. Bound by love's mercy, God is obliged by divinity's nature to fill with goodness creatures destined to be sacraments of mercy.

Created to be like God, we too are obliged to lavish mercy generously upon others. It is by this law that we will be judged. St. Augustine writes, "Those . . . who were willing to show mercy will be judged with mercy . . . and [God] reckons to their account their works of mercy: 'For I was hungry and you gave me to eat; I was thirsty and you gave me to drink' " (St. Augustine, bishop).[242]

We are stewards—dispensers—of God's mercy. The "great things" God has done for us are the fruits of mercy that we have been commissioned to extend to all who hunger and thirst for its goodness. "Of whose mercy," asks St. Augustine, "if not [God's]? If you were to give of your own, it would be largess; but since you give of [God's], it is restitution. 'For what have you that you have not received?' "[243]

QUESTION FOR YOUR REFLECTION

What is the natural law that obliges God?

WORD

"The second death has no power over them" (St. Fulgentius of Ruspe, bishop).[244]

REFLECTION

"Everyone wants to go to heaven but no one wants to die." These words of a song are especially correct when the first of two deaths in this life is absent. If Christians are faithful to their name, they embrace two deaths before sharing the resurrection of each.

The first death is conversion. It turns us around from this world's definition of human life and directs us to a purpose justified by faith. Conversion is the experience of passover from this world's purpose for human life to God's. We die to one, we are raised to the other.

If conversion's death is experienced, the death ending our tenure on earth need not be feared. All who root themselves in Christ and live his way, his truth, and his life pass over to an existence radically different, but so radically peaceful. "Later on," writes St. Fulgentius of Ruspe, "through bodily resurrection, the transformation of the just will be brought to completion, and they will experience a perfect, abiding, unchangeable glorification. The purpose of the change . . . is that they may abide in an eternal, changeless joy."[245]

All who sincerely seek the forgiveness that opens the way to holiness seek also conversion's "second death [that] has no power over them." For those who experience conversion, it is not true that "no one wants to die."

QUESTION FOR YOUR REFLECTION

What is the prime requisite for a happy death?

TUESDAY

WORD

"Receive him, for he took upon himself all that belongs to us except sin, to consume what is ours in what is his" (St. Andrew of Crete, bishop).[246]

REFLECTION

The depth of holiness is gauged by the forgiveness with which sinners have been raised from conversion's death.

196

In the home of a Pharisee, Jesus welcomes "a woman known in the town to be a sinner" as she wipes with her hair tears of repentance that bathe his feet (see Luke 7:37-50). The goodness of Christ also reaches out with forgiveness to an adulteress about to be put to death for a life of sin. Is this the Mary Magdalene to whom Jesus "first appeared" (Mark 16:9) on the day of his resurrection?

The acknowledgment of unworthiness qualifies us for companionship with Christ. Not to acknowledge Christ's presence on the basis of our unworthiness is a pride masked behind false humility. The only thing we can give to God that God does not possess is our sinfulness. In exchange, there is companionship with Christ. "God made him who did not know sin, to be sin, so that in him we might become the very holiness of God" (2 Cor 5:21).

QUESTION FOR YOUR REFLECTION

What is false humility?

WEDNESDAY

WORD

"How can we rejoice in the Lord if he is far from us? Pray God he may not be far. If he is, that is your doing" (St. Augustine, bishop).[247]

REFLECTION

In my Advent book, *God Is with Us,* I ask: "If God doesn't seem close to you, who moved?"[248]

St. Augustine responds, "That is your doing." We move away from God when our search for happiness detours to the lesser gods, whose bounty is "lewd conduct, impurity, licentiousness, idolatry, sorcery, hostilities, bickering, jealousy, outbursts of rage, selfish rivalries, dissensions, factions, envy, drunkenness, orgies, and the like" (Gal 5:19-21).

But "God is with us" when we have been led by God's Spirit to experience the bounty of God's presence: "love, joy, peace, patient endurance, kindness, generosity, faith, mildness, and chastity" (Gal 5:22-23).

The judgment of God's presence is discerned by the presence of the Holy Spirit's "first fruits" within us. St. Augustine writes, "Already we have the first fruits of the Spirit. . . . For we are drawing near to the one we love and not only are we drawing near—we even have some slight feeling and taste of the banquet we shall eagerly eat and drink."[249]

If "taste" for that "banquet" seems far away, who moved?

QUESTION FOR YOUR REFLECTION

How can we discern that "God is with us"?

THURSDAY

WORD

"On that day I will make Jerusalem a weighty stone for all peoples" (Zech 12:3).

REFLECTION

Jesus is saddened when he notices people "speaking of how the temple was adorned with precious stones and votive offerings." He says, " 'These things you are contemplating—the day will come when not one stone will be left on another, but it will all be torn down' " (Luke 21:5-6). The weight placed on this world's "precious stones" falls far short of the "really valuable pearl" with which Jesus' presence adorns humanity. This pearl is the "weighty stone" of integrity.

God's love is the weight of God's glory. The Son of God is with us to exchange his love for our destiny of being sacraments of God's love. This "weighty stone" is humanity's glory.

This glory cannot be purchased except by the love Christ revealed when he died on the cross. "The hour has come," he said, "for the Son of Man to be glorified. I solemnly assure you, unless the grain of wheat falls to the earth and dies, it remains just a grain of wheat. But if it dies, it produces much fruit" (John 12:23-24).

No one can lift the "weighty stone" of the cross except those who "proclaim the death of the Lord until he comes" (1 Cor 11:26). "No greater love can be conceived than this," St. Gregory of Nyssa asserts, "that you should purchase . . . salvation at the cost of your life."[250]

QUESTION FOR YOUR REFLECTION

What is the "cost of your life"?

FRIDAY

WORD

"We must strive to follow and fulfill in ourselves the various stages of Christ's plan as well as his mysteries, and frequently beg him to bring them to completion in us and in the whole Church" (St. John Eudes, priest).[251]

REFLECTION

We are "earthen vessels" (2 Cor 4:7) within whom the treasury of God's mysteries lie hidden. These mysteries await our consent "to bring them to completion in us and in the whole Church."

St. Paul writes: "It is not ourselves we preach but Christ Jesus as Lord. . . . For God, who said, 'Let light shine out of darkness,' has shone in our hearts, that we in turn might make known the glory of God shining on the face of Christ. This treasure we possess in earthen vessels, to make it clear that its surpassing power comes from God and not from us. . . . Continually we carry about in our bodies the dying of Jesus, so that in our bodies the life of Jesus may also be revealed" (2 Cor 4:5-7, 10).

When we admit that we are "earthen vessels," such humility qualifies us to be effective witnesses of Christ's light. Humility opens mystery's door to reveal the light of Christ, "the glory of God shining on the face of Christ." This is the light hidden in the bread and wine of the Eucharist seeking visibility in the "earthen vessels" of communicants. It is the light that begs visibility from Mary's humble surrender to God's will, a surrender that moves her to proclaim, "I am the servant of the Lord. Let it be done to me as you say" (Luke 1:38).

QUESTION FOR YOUR REFLECTION

There is no contradiction between Christ as "already" revealed and Christ as "not yet" revealed. Why?

WORD

"[Eternal life] consists in the complete satisfaction of desire, for there the blessed will be given more than they wanted" (St. Thomas Aquinas, priest).[252]

REFLECTION

Some people who daily fill themselves with food are slowly starving. They starve because their pursuit of one satisfaction permits them to ignore the pursuit of another. When they prefer being filled to being healthy, they court starvation.

On a deeper level the craving for lesser gods silences the craving to embrace God's wholeness. This craving appears again and again even when other cravings have been met. It reappears because hearts created for God's companionship cannot be at peace with gods whose peace has limited tenure.

St. Thomas Aquinas writes: "The reason . . . that in this life no one can fulfill his longing [is because] only God satisfies . . . all other pleasures. That is why man can rest in nothing but God. As St. Augustine says, 'You have made us for yourself, Lord, and our heart can find no rest until it rests in you.' "[253]

QUESTION FOR YOUR REFLECTION

What hunger is left unattended among some of the well-fed?

Thirty-fourth Week in Ordinary Time

WORD

"It is clear that he who prays for the coming of God's kingdom prays rightly to have it within himself, that there it might grow and bear fruit. For God reigns in each of his holy ones" (Origen, priest).[254]

REFLECTION

The kingdom of God does not begin when we enter heaven "up there." The kingdom of God, Jesus says, "is already in your midst" (Luke 17:21).

But we do pray "Your kingdom come" (Matt 6:10). The kingdom comes when it is seen in the lives of people who live by the rule of Jesus Christ. When his rule can be seen in those whose lives are in sharp contrast to the lives of those who live by the rules of this world, the kingdom of God has come.

The kingdom of heaven is within those who live by justice leading to peace, by responsibility leading to freedom, and by grace leading to integrity. Everyone possesses the capacity to live by this rule and so to show clearly that they have tasted the presence of God's kingdom here on earth as it is in heaven. Those who exercise this capacity become disciples whose lives display the justice, peace, responsibility, freedom, and integrity that are signs of God's kingdom within them.

Christ the King is enthroned in disciples whose rule of life bears the imprint of Christ's identity. Origin writes: "There should be in us a kind of spiritual paradise where God may walk and be our sole ruler with his Christ. In us the Lord will sit at the right hand of that spiritual power we wish to receive. And he will sit there until all his enemies who are within us become his 'footstool,' and every principality . . . in us is cast out."[255]

QUESTION FOR YOUR REFLECTION

When does the reign of Christ the King begin in each of us?

WORD

> *"There are many kinds of wealth and a variety of grounds for rejoicing; every [person's] treasure is that which he desires"* (St. Leo the Great, pope).[256]

REFLECTION

"Remember," Jesus cautions, "where your treasure is, there your heart is also" (Matt 6:21). When Jesus Christ is the "treasure" that justifies the reason for living, the hearts of Christians are in the right place. If there is consistency between our words about Jesus and his integration into our identity, such integrity speaks of a great heart. Wholeness radiates from hearts that treasure Christ revealing the holiness that springs from the heart of Christ.

If we treasure knowledge *about* Christ we may not be wholly in communion with him, the treasure that surpasses even knowledge of encyclopedic dimension. "I tell you," Jesus declares, "unless your holiness surpasses that of the scribes and Pharisees you shall not enter the kingdom of God" (Matt 5:20).

Encyclopedic though it be, knowledge about Christ can never bear the fruit of communion with him and with one another. Holiness springs from hearts that treasure the desire to share Christ's identity. This desire is every heart's knowledge, treasured by all "who hunger and thirst for holiness" (Matt 5:6).

Hearts that "hunger and thirst for holiness" treasure Christ's own hunger and thirst. They long to be filled with "everything necessary for a life of genuine piety, through knowledge of him who called us by his own glory and power . . ." to "become sharers of the divine nature" (2 Pet 1:3-4). Yes, "every [person's] treasure is that which he desires" because such hearts are the treasure that God desires.

QUESTION FOR YOUR REFLECTION

A test for what your heart most treasures: About what do you think and talk, and with what do you spend most of each day?

TUESDAY

WORD

"We possess the prophetic message as something altogether reliable" (2 Pet 1:19).

REFLECTION

On earth, we rely on the testimony of our five senses. They have the companionship of faith calling them to accept as "altogether reliable" its testimony that earthly life is not one's final destiny. This companionship is spurious when faith alone claims entry into the human spirit without the fellowship of sense experience.

St. Peter writes: "It was not by way of cleverly concocted myths that we taught you about the coming in power of our Lord Jesus Christ, for we were eyewitnesses of his sovereign majesty. He received glory and praise from God the Father when that unique declaration came to him out of the majestic splendor: 'This is my beloved Son, on whom my favor rests.' We ourselves heard this said from heaven while we were in his company on the holy mountain" (2 Pet 1:16-18).

Body and soul are one. For this reason "the Word became flesh" (John 1:14), enabling God's "prophetic message" to be received "as something altogether reliable." The Church is reliable because its human and divine identity mirrors Christ's. This identity is its credential for reliability.

When life's tenure on earth is ended, so ends the companionship of faith and sense experience. Their testimony pales before the testimony of seeing God face to face. Where on earth can be found any more reliable testimony than this?

203

QUESTION FOR YOUR REFLECTION

How are sacraments signs of faith's companionship with our five senses?

WORD

> *"[Christ] assumed a body, and using the cross as his plow-share cultivated the barren soul of man"* (St. Macarius, bishop).[257]

REFLECTION

We live in tension. We live in the world for a fruitfulness harvested by another. What we see and experience is the tillage; what we believe is the harvest. We are a soil to be tilled now; faith's prophetic message concerns the soil's harvest.

What is the instrument of our tillage? St. Macarius writes: "Christ our heavenly king came to till the soil of mankind devastated by sin. He assumed a body and, using the cross as his plowshare, cultivated the barren soul of man. . . . And when he had plowed the soul with the wood of the cross, he planted in it a most lovely garden of the Spirit that could produce for its Lord and God the sweetest and most pleasant fruit of every kind."[258]

In the "soil" of our lives "plowed" by the seeds of suffering, the seeds of resurrection are also planted. In the midst of pain we meet Christ, who continues to complete what he began on the cross (*see* Col 1:24). We also meet Christ who seeks from us the completion of resurrection, begun when his Father raised him from the tomb. He who had been emptied of his heavenly reign was raised so that we who had been emptied of human dignity in Eden's garden might be raised with him.

Is suffering futile? Not if the seeds of Christ's resurrection have been planted in the soil of suffering. "Those that sow in tears shall reap rejoicing" (Ps 126:5).

QUESTION FOR YOUR REFLECTION

Why is euthanasia a blindness to the meaning of Christ's death and resurrection?

THURSDAY

WORD

"They promise . . . freedom though they themselves are slaves of corruption—for surely anyone is the slave of that by which he has been overcome" (2 Pet 2:19).

REFLECTION

Every sin flows from the lie that the choice of this world's goodness guarantees ultimate happiness. When this deception rules one's life, freedom becomes license to do whatever one chooses. Those who live by this license are enslaved by their choices.

Lust lies hidden in this deception. It contains the lie that a particular good is the whole good enthroned at human life's center. The fruit of this lie is addiction, leading the addicted to discover that they have been conned into becoming clones of their lust.

Choice's sacredness is not derived from the freedom to do whatever one pleases. Choice is sacred because it is rooted in God's choice of purpose for all men and women. God creates us to *be* like God and *act* accordingly. "Remember," St. Paul says, "that you have been called to live in freedom—but not a freedom that gives free rein to the flesh. Out of love, place yourselves at one another's service. The whole law has found its fulfillment in this one saying: 'You shall love your neighbor as yourself'" (Gal 5:13-14).

People are not deceived when they love themselves for their likeness to God; neither are they deceived when the love forming that likeness urges them to love others.

QUESTION FOR YOUR REFLECTION

There is the axiom that what one does flows from who one is. Which of the two guarantees sacredness to freedom of choice?

WORD

"Our obligation is to do God's will, and not our own" (St. Cyprian, bishop).[259]

REFLECTION

God's will is timeless. It links the past, the present, and the future. "This point," St. Peter writes, "must not be overlooked. . . . In the Lord's eyes, one day is as a thousand years and a thousand years are as a day" (2 Pet 3:8).

The timeless will of God is communion with all of us. Jesus expresses God's longing for communion when he prays "that all may be one as you, Father, are in me, and I in you; I pray that they may be [one] in us, that the world may believe that you sent me" (John 17:21). With utter simplicity, Jesus utters the will of God.

God longs that we be consumed by that same longing. Like fire, it is a longing that destroys all other desires that prevent the reality of communion with God. The fire of God's longing is at the Church's beginning and has never ceased burning with the longing for us "to do God's will, and not our own."

"The world hates Christians," St. Cyprian insists, "so why give your love to it instead of following Christ? . . . 'Never give your love to the world' [St. John warns], 'or to anything in it. A man cannot love the Father and love the world at the same time. All that the world offers is the lust of the flesh, the lust of the eyes and earthly ambition. The world will pass away, but the [one] who has done the will of God shall live forever.' "[260]

QUESTION FOR YOUR REFLECTION

What is the will of God and how do we know it is alive within us?

WORD

"Let us sing alleluia here on earth, while we still live in anxiety, so that we may sing it one day in heaven in full security" (St. Augustine, bishop).[261]

REFLECTION

Alleluia links us to heaven, for though we sing it "in anxiety," it joyfully rings from a faith that joins us to heaven's security.

Of necessity we sing with anxiety. We are anxious not because we mistrust God but because we mistrust ourselves. St. Augustine asks, "Do you want to feel secure when I am daily asking pardon for my sins, and requesting help in time of trial?"[262]

We are tried so that we might experience the security of God's faithfulness. Its imprint is made possible by our faith, whereby we may "grow strong . . . through prayer in the Holy Spirit" (Jude 20). In exchange for trials faith persuades us that God is faithful, a persuasion that breaks out in heaven's "alleluia."

Each of us is a "little out of the ordinary." From that littleness God invests heaven with our graced littleness. How little, then, is the test of ordinary time when such a marvelous exchange is already taking place! It is in the light of this exchange that St. Augustine sings:

O the happiness of the heavenly alleluia! . . . God's praises are sung both there and here, but here they are sung in anxiety, there in security; here they are sung by those destined to die, there, by those destined to live forever; here they are sung in hope, there, in hope's fulfillment; here they are sung by wayfarers, there, by those living in their own country.[263]

Alleluia!

QUESTION FOR YOUR REFLECTION

Why does God try us?

Notes

1. "Letter to the Corinthians," Funk. See *Liturgy of the Hours* 3:55.
2. Ibid.
3. "Detailed Rules for Monks," *Patrologia Graeca.* See *Liturgy of the Hours* 3:60.
4. Ibid., 59.
5. "Against Heresies," *Sources Chrétiennes.* See *Liturgy of the Hours* 3:63.
6. Ibid.
7. "Discourse Against the Pagans," *Patrologia Graeca.* See *Liturgy of the Hours* 3:68.
8. Ibid., 71–72.
9. "Letter to the Corinthians," Funk. See *Liturgy of the Hours* 3:76.
10. "Letter to the Ephesians," Funk. See *Liturgy of the Hours* 3:80.
11. Ibid., 84.
12. "A Letter," *Corpus Christianorum, Series Latina.* See *Liturgy of the Hours* 3:97.
13. Ibid.
14. "On Spiritual Perfection," *Patrologia Graeca.* See *Liturgy of the Hours* 3:101.
15. Ibid., 102.
16. "Treatise Against the Heresies," *Sources Chrétiennes.* See *Liturgy of the Hours* 3:105.
17. "The Constitution on the Sacred Liturgy." See *Liturgy of the Hours* 3:110.
18. *The Sacramentary* (Collegeville: The Liturgical Press, 1985).
19. "Pastoral Constitution on the Church in the Modern World." See *Liturgy of the Hours* 3:116.
20. "Detailed Rules for Monks," *Patrologia Graeca.* See *Liturgy of the Hours* 3:120.
21. "Sermon on the Song of Songs," *Opera Omnia.* See *Liturgy of the Hours* 3:125.
22. *The Sacramentary* (Collegeville: The Liturgical Press, 1985).

23. "A Sermon," *Patrologia Latina Supplementum.* See *Liturgy of the Hours* 3:129.

24. Ibid., 130.

25. "Sacrament of Penance Study," *Origins* 19, no. 38 (1990) 621.

26. No. 18. See *Liturgy of the Hours* 3:137.

27. *On Evangelization in the Modern World,* no. 41 (Washington: United States Catholic Conference, 1976) 28.

28. "Commentary on the Psalms," *Patrologia Latina Supplementum.* See *Liturgy of the Hours* 3:147.

29. Walter M. Abbott, ed., *The Documents of Vatican II,* "Dogmatic Constitution on the Church," no. 1 (New York: The America Press, 1966).

30. "Against Heresies," *Sources Chrétiennes.* See *Liturgy of the Hours* 3:151.

31. "On Spiritual Perfection," *Patrologia Graeca.* See *Liturgy of the Hours* 3:154.

32. Ibid.

33. "From a Homily by a Spiritual Writer of the Fourth Century," *Patrologia Graeca.* See *Liturgy of the Hours* 3:162.

34. Ibid., 163.

35. "Explanation of Paul's Letter to the Galatians," *Patrologia Latina.* See *Liturgy of the Hours* 3:170.

36. "A Short Discourse," *Opera Omnia.* See *Liturgy of the Hours* 3:174.

37. Ibid.

38. "Sermon on the Nativity of the Lord," *Patrologia Latina.* See *Liturgy of the Hours* 3:191-192.

39. "Commentary on the Diatessaron," *Sources Chrétiennes.* See *Liturgy of the Hours* 3:200.

40. "Sermon," *Patrologia Latina.* See *Liturgy of the Hours* 3:204.

41. Ibid., 203.

42. "Discourse Against the Arians," *Patrologia Graeca.* See *Liturgy of the Hours* 3:208.

43. "Explanation of the Psalms," *Corpus Scriptorum Ecclesiasticorum Latinorum.* See *Liturgy of the Hours* 3:216.

44. Ibid.

45. "The Tractates on the First Letter of John," *Patrologia Latina.* See *Liturgy of the Hours* 3:220.

46. Ibid.

47. "Pastoral Constitution on the Church in the Modern World." See *Liturgy of the Hours* 3:224.

48. "Homily on Ecclesiastes," *Patrologia Graeca.* See *Liturgy of the Hours* 3:234.

49. Anthony de Mello, *Song of the Bird* (Chicago: Loyola University Press, 1983) 170.

50. "Instruction on Faith," *Opera.* See *Liturgy of the Hours* 3:247.

51. Ibid., 246.

52. "A Commentary on Ecclesiastes," *Patrologia Graeca.* See *Liturgy of the Hours* 3:251.

53. Ibid, 256.

54. *Daily Readings with St. John of the Cross* (Springfield, Ill: Templegate, 1985) 21.

55. "Moral Reflections on Job," *Patrologia Latina.* See *Liturgy of the Hours* 3:265.

56. "Confessions," *Corpus Scriptorum Ecclesiasticorum Latinorum.* See *Liturgy of the Hours* 3:269.

57. Ibid., 273.

58. Ibid.

59. "The Hound of Heaven." See *Liturgy of the Hours,* Appendix, 3:1989.

60. *On Evangelization in the Modern World,* no. 21 (Washington: United States Catholic Conference, 1976) 17.

61. "The Teachings," *Patrologia Graeca.* See *Liturgy of the Hours* 3:300.

62. "Moral Reflections," *Patrologia Latina.* See *Liturgy of the Hours* 3:304.

63. Ibid., 304–305.

64. Ibid., 308.

65. "Sermon," *Patrologia Latina.* See *Liturgy of the Hours* 3:312.

66. "Exposition on John." See *Liturgy of the Hours* 3:315.

67. Ibid., 316.

68. "Letter to the Romans," Funk. See *Liturgy of the Hours* 3:321.

69. Ibid.

70. Ibid., 324.

71. Ibid., 329.

72. Ibid., 330.

73. Robert Frost, *The Poetry of Robert Frost* (New York: Holt, Rinehart and Winston, 1961).

74. "Homily on Joshua," *Patrologia Graeca.* See *Liturgy of the Hours* 3:334.

75. Ibid., 338.

76. "Explanations of the Psalms," *Corpus Scriptorum Ecclesiasticorum Latinorum.* See *Liturgy of the Hours* 3:344.

77. "Treatise on the Lord's Prayer," *Corpus Scriptorum Ecclesiasticorum Latinorum.* See *Liturgy of the Hours* 3:352.

78. Ibid., 358.

79. Democracy in America (New York: Doubleday/Anchor Books, 1969) 506.

80. "Treatise on the Lord's Prayer," *Corpus Scriptorum Ecclesiasticorum Latinorum.* See *Liturgy of the Hours* 3:358.

81. Ibid., 363.

82. Ibid., 367.

83. Ibid., 371.

84. Ibid., 376.

85. "Treatise on Human Perfection," *Patrologia Graeca.* See *Liturgy of the Hours* 3:395.

86. "Treatise on Spiritual Friendship," *Patrologia Latina.* See *Liturgy of the Hours* 3:399.

87. "Homily on the Beatitudes," *Patrologia Graeca.* See *Liturgy of the Hours* 3:403.

88. "God's Grandeur." See *Liturgy of the Hours,* Appendix 4, 3:1985.

89. "Homily on the Beatitudes," *Patrologia Graeca.* See *Liturgy of the Hours* 3:408.

90. Ibid., 407.

91. Ibid., 413.

92. "Sermon," *Corpus Christianorum, Series Latina.* See *Liturgy of the Hours* 3:426.

93. "The Way of Perfection." See *Liturgy of the Hours* 3:431.

94. "Sermon on Psalm 41," *Corpus Christianorum, Series Latina.* See *Liturgy of the Hours* 3:435.

95. "Catechetical Instruction," *Patrologia Graeca.* See *Liturgy of the Hours* 3:445.

96. "Sermon," *Corpus Christianorum, Series Latina.* See *Liturgy of the Hours* 3:451.

97. Ibid.

98. "Letter to the Corinthians," Funk. See *Liturgy of the Hours* 3:456.

99. "Discourse on the Psalms," *Corpus Christianorum, Series Latina,* Funk. See *Liturgy of the Hours* 3:460.

100. Funk. See *Liturgy of the Hours* 3:465.

101. "Exposition of Psalm 118," *Corpus Scriptorum Ecclesiasticorum Latinorum.* See *Liturgy of the Hours* 3:469.

102. Ibid.

103. "Letter to the Corinthians," Funk. See *Liturgy of the Hours* 3:473.

104. "Discourse on the Psalms," *Corpus Christianorum, Series Latina.* See *Liturgy of the Hours* 3:477.

105. "On the Mysteries," *Sources Chrétiennes.* See *Liturgy of the Hours* 3:491.

106. William Zinsser, *Writing to Learn* (New York, Harper & Row, 1988).

107. "On the Mysteries," *Sources Chrétiennes.* See *Liturgy of the Hours* 3:496.

108. Ibid., 497.

109. Ibid., 503.

110. Randall Balmer, "Competing in Free Market of Religion" (Des Moines: *Register* (May 20, 1991).

111. "On the Mysteries," *Sources Chrétiennes* 3:512.

112. "Letter to the Magnesians," Funk. See *Liturgy of the Hours* 3:520.

113. *On Evangelization in the Modern World,* no. 41 (Washington: United States Catholic Conference, 1976) 28.

114. See *Liturgy of the Hours* 3:527, 528.

115. Ibid.

116. "Explanations of the Psalms," *Corpus Scriptorum Ecclesiasticorum Latinorum.* See *Liturgy of the Hours* 3:531.

117. "Centesimus Annus," *Origins* 21:1 (May 16, 1991) no. 11.

118. "Sermon," *Corpus Christianorum, Series Latina.* See *Liturgy of the Hours* 3:547.

119. "Sermon on Charity," *Patrologia Graeca.* See *Liturgy of the Hours* 3:552.

120. "Catechetical Instruction," *Patrologia Graeca.* See *Liturgy of the Hours* 3:560.

121. *The Sacramentary* (Collegeville: The Liturgical Press, 1985).

122. "Letter to St. Polycarp," Funk. See *Liturgy of the Hours* 3:564.

123. Ibid., 568.

124. Robert W. McElroy, *The Search for an American Public Theology* (New York: Paulist, 1988) 169.

125. "A Letter Attributed to Barnabas," Funk. See *Liturgy of the Hours* 4:56.

126. Ibid., 61.

127. Ibid., 71.

128. Ibid., 72.

129. "A Treatise," *Patrologia Latina.* See *Liturgy of the Hours* 4:76.

130. Leonard Foley, *Saint of the Day* (Cincinnati: St. Anthony Messenger Press, 1990) 201.

131. "A Treatise," *Patrologia Latina.* See *Liturgy of the Hours* 4:75.

132. "Spiritual Canticle." See *Liturgy of the Hours* 4:81.

133. Ibid., 80–81.

134. Preface of Sundays in Ordinary Time VII, *The Sacramentary* (Collegeville: The Liturgical Press, 1985).

135. "Treatise Against Heresies," *Sources Chrétiennes.* See *Liturgy of the Hours* 4:85.

136. "On Divine Providence." See *Liturgy of the Hours* 4:90.

137. Ibid.

138. "On the Incarnation of the Lord," *Patrologia Graeca.* See *Liturgy of the Hours* 4:94, 95.

139. Ibid.

140. Ibid., 99.

141. "Christian Perfection," *Patrologia Graeca.* See *Liturgy of the Hours* 4:106.

142. Preface of Sundays in Ordinary Time VII, *The Sacramentary* (Collegeville: The Liturgical Press, 1985).

143. "Sermon on Baptism," *Patrologia Latina.* See *Liturgy of the Hours* 4:115.

144. Preface of Christian Death I, *The Sacramentary* (Collegeville: The Liturgical Press, 1985).

145. Eucharistic Prayers II and III, *The Sacramentary.*

146. "Moral Reflections on Job," *Patrologia Latina*. See *Liturgy of the Hours* 4:127.

147. "Sermon," *Patrologia Latina Supplementum*. See *Liturgy of the Hours* 4:134.

148. "Explanation of the Psalms," *Corpus Scriptorum Ecclesiasticorum Latinorum*. See *Liturgy of the Hours* 4:148.

149. "The Pastoral Constitution on the Church in the Modern World." See *Liturgy of the Hours* 4:153.

150. "Homily," *Patrologia Graeca*. See *Liturgy of the Hours* 4:162.

151. Ibid.

152. Ibid.

153. Ibid., 163.

154. Ibid.

155. Ibid.

156. "An Instruction Concerning Christ the Font of Life," *Opera*. See *Liturgy of the Hours* 4:168.

157. Ibid., 174.

158. "A Commentary," *Patrologia Latina*. See *Liturgy of the Hours* 4:178.

159. "A Homily on Matthew," *Patrologia Graeca*. See *Liturgy of the Hours* 4:182.

160. "A Sermon," *Corpus Christianorum, Series Latina*. See *Liturgy of the Hours* 4:188.

161. Ibid.

162. See *Liturgy of the Hours* 4:194.

163. "Commentary on John," *Patrologia Graeca*. See *Liturgy of the Hours* 4:202.

164. "A Sermon on the Beatitudes," *Patrologia Latina*. See *Liturgy of the Hours* 4:207.

165. Ibid., 210–211.

166. Ibid., 216.

167. Ibid., 222.

168. Ibid., 226.

169. "A Sermon," *Opera Omnia*. See *Liturgy of the Hours* 4:235.

170. "Discourse on the Psalms." See *Liturgy of the Hours* 4:241.

171. Ibid.

172. Robert Frost, *The Poetry of Robert Frost* (New York: Holt, Rinehart and Winston, 1961).

173. "Sermon," *Patrologia Latina*. See *Liturgy of the Hours* 4:246-247.

174. "Sermon," *Patrologia Graeca*. See *Liturgy of the Hours* 4:250.

175. "Sermon on Pastors," *Corpus Christianorum, Series Latina*. See *Liturgy of the Hours* 4:255.

176. *On Evangelization in the Modern World,* no. 41 (Washington: United States Catholic Conference, 1976) 28.

177. "Sermon On Pastors," *Corpus Christianorum, Series Latina.* See *Liturgy of the Hours* 4:263-265.

178. Ibid.

179. Ibid., 271.

180. Ibid., 277.

181. Ibid., 276.

182. Ibid., 281.

183. Ibid., 286.

184. Ibid., 290–291.

185. Ibid., 295.

186. Ibid., 300–307.

187. "Discourse on the Psalms," *Corpus Scriptorum Ecclesiasticorum Latinorum.* See *Liturgy of the Hours* 4:311.

188. "A letter to the Philippians," Funk. See *Liturgy of the Hours* 4:315.

189. Ibid., 327.

190. "Treatise on the Letter to the Philippians," *Patrologia Latina Supplementum.* See *Liturgy of the Hours* 4:334.

191. "Christian Formation," *Patrologia Graeca.* See *Liturgy of the Hours* 4:339.

192. "A Treatise on Cain and Abel," *Corpus Scriptorum Ecclesiasticorum Latinorum.* See *Liturgy of the Hours* 4:347.

193. "A Letter to the Trallians," Funk. See *Liturgy of the Hours* 4:356.

194. "A letter to the Philadelphians," Funk. See *Liturgy of the Hours* 4:361.

195. "The First Instruction," *Patrologia Latina.* See *Liturgy of the Hours* 4:363.

196. Walter M. Abbott, ed., *The Documents of Vatican II,* "Dogmatic Constitution on Divine Revelation," no. 8.

197. "The First Instruction," *Patrologia Latina.* See *Liturgy of the Hours* 4:364-365.

198. "A Homily on the Gospels," *Patrologia Latina.* See *Liturgy of the Hours* 4:367-368.

199. "An Instruction," *Opera.* See *Liturgy of the Hours* 4:383.

200. "Inquiry Addressed to Thalassius," *Patrologia Graeca.* See *Liturgy of the Hours* 4:386, 387.

201. "Treatise on John," *Corpus Christianorum, Series Latina.* See *Liturgy of the Hours* 4:391.

202. Ibid., 392.

203. Ibid.

204. "The City of God," *Corpus Christianorum, Series Latina.* See *Liturgy of the Hours* 4:397.

205. No. 45. See *Liturgy of the Hours* 4:404.

206. *The Sacramentary* (Collegeville: The Liturgical Press, 1985).

207. "Letter to Proba," *Corpus Scriptorum Ecclesiasticorum Latinorum.* See *Liturgy of the Hours* 4:408.

208. Ibid.

209. Ibid., 412.

210. Ibid., 417.

211. Ibid., 421.

212. Alden Hatch, *Crown of Glory* (New York: Hawthorne, 1957) 65.

213. "Letter to Proba," *Corpus Scriptorum Ecclesiasticorum Latinorum*. See *Liturgy of the Hours* 4:425.

214. Ibid., 430.

215. "Letter to the Corinthians," Funk. See *Liturgy of the Hours* 4:439.

216. Ibid.

217. Ibid., 448.

218. "A Discourse Against the Arians," *Patrologia Graeca*. See *Liturgy of the Hours* 4:456.

219. "A Word by Baldwin," *Patrologia Latina*. See *Liturgy of the Hours* 4:461.

220. Ibid., 461–462.

221. *The Sacramentary* (Collegeville: The Liturgical Press, 1985).

222. "A Dialogue on Divine Providence." See *Liturgy of the Hours* 4:466.

223. No. 78. See *Liturgy of the Hours* 4:471.

224. Ibid., nos. 82–83, 476.

225. Ibid.

226. Ibid., nos. 88–90, 480.

227. "A Catechetical Instruction," *Patrologia Graeca*. See *Liturgy of the Hours* 4:485.

228. Ibid., 488.

229. Ibid., 489.

230. Ibid.

231. *The Sacramentary* (Collegeville: The Liturgical Press, 1985).

232. "A Catechetical Instruction," *Patrologia Graeca*. See *Liturgy of the Hours* 4:493.

233. "Treatise on Death as a Blessing," *Corpus Scriptorum Ecclesiasticorum Latinorum*. See *Liturgy of the Hours* 4:497.

234. *The Sacramentary* (Collegeville: The Liturgical Press, 1985).

235. "A Homily Written in the Second Century," Funk. See *Liturgy of the Hours* 4:513.

236. Ibid., 521.

237. Ibid.

238. Ibid., 522.

239. Ibid., 526.

240. Ibid.

241. Ibid., 530.

242. "A Discourse on the Psalms," *Corpus Christianorum, Series Latina*. See *Liturgy of the Hours* 4:536.

243. Ibid.

244. "Treatise on Forgiveness," *Corpus Christianorum, Series Latina*. See *Liturgy of the Hours* 4:541.

245. Ibid.

246. "A Discourse," *Patrologia Graeca*. See *Liturgy of the Hours* 4:546.

247. "A Sermon," *Corpus Christianorum, Series Latina*. See *Liturgy of the Hours* 4:551.

248. John J. McIlhon, *God Is With Us* (Collegeville: The Liturgical Press, 1989) 9.

249. "A Sermon," *Corpus Christianorum, Series Latina*. See *Liturgy of the Hours* 4:551.

250. "A Commentary on the Song of Songs," *Patrologia Graeca*. See *Liturgy of the Hours* 4:555.

251. "Treatise on the Kingdom of Jesus," *Opera Omnia*. See *Liturgy of the Hours* 4:559.

252. "A Conference on 'I Believe in God,'" *Opuscula Theologica*. See *Liturgy of the Hours* 4:564.

253. Ibid.

254. "A Notebook on Prayer," *Patrologia Graeca*. See *Liturgy of the Hours* 4:576.

255. Ibid., 577.

256. "A Sermon," *Patrologia Latina*. See *Liturgy of the Hours* 4:589.

257. "A Homily," *Patrologia Graeca*. See *Liturgy of the Hours* 4:596.

258. Ibid.

259. "Sermon on Man's Mortality," *Corpus Scriptorum Ecclesiasticorum Latinorum*. See *Liturgy of the Hours* 4:603.

260. Ibid., 604.

261. "Sermon," *Patrologia Latina*. See *Liturgy of the Hours* 4:608.

262. Ibid.

263. Ibid., 609.